allabout
books

All About
Birds

By Robert S. Lemmon

Illustrated by Fritz Kredel

RANDOM HOUSE
NEW YORK

Library of Congress Catalog Card Number: 55-9513

Dewey Decimal Classification: 598.2

Contents

Foreword

Here is a different kind of book about birds! And one that is very exciting!

I have read dozens of bird books but have never seen one like this for young people. Most of the books are devoted largely to identifying birds; Bob Lemmon introduces you to the bird's world—where it lives, how it flies, why it migrates, the secrets of its feathers and its eggs.

After you read this book, you will look at birds through different eyes. You will marvel at their adaptations—the sharp talons of the osprey, the long probing bill of the hummingbird, the tail feathers that brace the woodpecker against a tree. These are fascinating things, and they are real!

I believe it was the great naturalist, Louis Agassiz, who, when asked how he had spent his vacation, replied, "I got nearly halfway across my back yard." Yes, there are many absorbing stories being unfolded in our own back yards and down the street in a vacant lot. It is a pity that so many of us have eyes but see not. Fortunate indeed are those who have their eyes opened to the pageant of nature that unfolds before us every day. It seems to me that *All About Birds* will do just that.

I am confident that after reading this book a great many people will want to take up bird study as a hobby. It is one of the most delightful avocations in the world. All you need is a sharp eye, a keen ear, and some curiosity about the world around you. For wherever you live there are birds whose lives unfold like a constantly changing drama. As you watch the birds and record their amazing habits, you will feel the joy and satisfaction that only a bird watcher can understand.

As I write these words, a house wren serenades me from his bird box just twenty feet away, goldfinches bounce around overhead, a wood thrush carols from the hillside, and two red-shouldered hawks are piercing the air with their strident but wildly beautiful cries. Perhaps they are trying to tell me that this is their valley as well as ours!

Make no mistake about it—bird study is an escape *into* reality, an open sesame to year-round pleasure.

KENNETH D. MORRISON
Editor, *Audubon Magazine*

How Many Birds Are There?

Nobody has actually counted every bird, of course, but people who study wild birds believe there are about one hundred billion of them in the whole world. Right here in the United States and Canada, there are around twelve or fifteen billion. That includes the sea gulls and other water birds which spend most of their time cruising along the Atlantic and Pacific coasts and out over the oceans.

This tremendous feathered crowd is so big that it

amounts to about fifty birds for every man, woman and child on the entire earth. It is made up of between eight and nine thousand distinct kinds of birds plus a large number of related kinds which are only slightly different. Between six and seven hundred species are living wild in our own country.

The biggest bird of all sometimes stands eight feet high and weighs three hundred pounds. That's the ostrich, of course. It really comes from Africa, but you often see it in our zoos. And the smallest bird is believed to be the tiny bee hummingbird of Cuba. It is only two inches long and weighs a good deal less than the letter on which you stick a three-cent stamp.

I don't suppose there is a single color you ever saw, or can think of, that isn't to be found in the feathers of one or another of these marvelous flying creatures. A few of them, like crows and white herons, have feathers that are all the same color on the outside. But underneath they may be a little different. In a great many others, the feathers show a dozen or more different colors and shades of colors. Even the bills of some birds, such as the toucans and puffins, are brighter and more showy than any rainbow. And finally, the eyes of certain kinds have such surprising colors as green and different shades of red, yellow, white and pink.

Maybe you are wondering why there are so many different sorts and sizes of birds spread all over the globe. One reason is that the world has a great number of different climates. For instance, the tropics are hot right through the year, but the arctic and antarctic have almost twelve months of bitter cold. The deserts are dry, and the big forests near the equator are wet. And each of these climates has its special sorts of trees and other plants. Since birds and many other wild creatures depend very largely on the kinds of things that grow around them, they too must have lots of differences of their own.

Many birds make their homes near lakes or marshes.

All About Birds

When you think about it, you can see why a bird which is used to living in Iceland could not get along in Panama. And one which is happy in the middle of the Arizona desert would be unable to live far out at sea as the albatross does.

Right in your own neighborhood you may have open fields, woods, lakes or rivers, mountains or marshes. If so, you will see that all have their special kinds of birds. They are not there just by accident. They are there because those are the surroundings in which they get along best. A great many of these birds have special sorts of bills, feet, or wings to help in the kinds of life they live.

It would take a long time and a lot of traveling to see every sort of bird in this country. But a surprising number of them can be found close to home.

For instance, if you live in a village or at the edge of a town, you can probably see at least fifty different kinds of birds at some time during the year. In some parts of the country there may be a hundred or more. Plenty of people who are good at identifying birds can go out on a pleasant spring morning and find well over a hundred species before nightfall. It just takes steady searching in the right places.

How Many Birds Are There?

Some of the birds you see will be more common than others, of course. If you count the total number of birds without bothering about what kinds they are, your list for the day may easily come to several hundred. Often, when winter has brought the big flocks of salt-water ducks down from the North, I have seen seven or eight thousand of just one species in a couple of hours along the New England coast.

It's fun to keep a notebook in which you put down the number of birds you see each time you go out. It is also interesting to record how many of each kind you see together with the date, temperature and something about the weather. You will be surprised to see how many there will be when you have had a little practice, and how greatly the list changes from one season to the other.

As you become familiar with more and more kinds of birds, you will realize that birds and their ways make up one of Nature's most wonderful stories.

The Oldest Bird in the World

If it were possible today to see the world's first bird, you would certainly be surprised. For it was a long, skinny creature with a bill full of teeth. Its backbone stuck out behind like the tail of a lizard. But it did have wings and real feathers. Some of the feathers grew all along each side of a long, many-boned tail, instead of being bunched together at the rear end of the body as in our present-day birds. Scientists believe this creature appeared in the Jurassic Period. That was about a hundred and thirty million years ago while a good many of the dinosaurs and huge flying reptiles were still alive. Scientists call this first bird *archaeopteryx*.

The Oldest Bird in the World

This oldest of all the birds vanished a long time before there were any people on earth. The only known record of archaeopteryx is some fossil bones and feathers buried in slate rock. They were found in Germany by Andreas Wagner, back in the year 1861. He had never seen anything like them. But scientists are able to determine the age of such things by studying the kinds of rocks in which they are found. Scientists went to work on Wagner's discovery and finally came up with a good idea of when the creature lived and what it must have looked like. Today the remains of those ancient feathers and bones are in the British Museum just as they were found hidden away in the slate.

At the time the archaeopteryx was alive, the world was occupied chiefly by the reptiles. Many of these four-legged, scaly beasts were somewhat like alligators and lizards of today. There were so many of them that men call that time the Age of Reptiles. A few million years earlier, some of these creatures had begun to wear scales that looked a little like feathers. After a long time those along the front legs grew quite slender and feathery. That was the first step toward the development of regular wings.

Many thousands of years passed and very, very

slowly other changes took place among this particular lot of reptiles that were on their way to becoming birds. Their front legs finally turned into bigger and better wings. All their bones became thinner and more filled with little air pockets. Thus, there was less weight to carry through the air. By that time many of these creatures were doing a lot of flying. So little by little their shoulder bones became stronger and changed shape in order to manage the wings better.

Larger flying muscles were needed to keep the wings flapping. For this reason the creatures' breastbones grew deeper and more keel-shaped to provide strong anchorage for the new muscles. Their hind legs got longer, too. This raised their bodies higher into the air so it became easier to take off in flight. The long, many-jointed tails got shorter and shorter. Finally they were just the few stubby little bones which make such a fine base for the sort of tail feathers birds have today.

Along with these big changes there were smaller ones just as interesting. For instance, the eyes of the reptile ancestors of birds were usually small and weak. Although their skulls were made up of many bones neatly fitted together, they didn't have much space for brains. That was poor equipment for a creature that was be-

Fossil remains of archaeopteryx were found buried in slate.

coming expert at flying around looking for food. Very gradually, these birds-to-be developed large, strong brain cases and much bigger and sharper eyes. As they became less and less like the reptiles and other four-legged animals, they began eating insects and other small, soft foods. So they had no further need for teeth and finally stopped growing them altogether.

Then, after many more years than you could count, most of the reptiles began to disappear. But those which had turned into birds kept growing stronger and stronger. Some of them became large and others small. Their feathers turned different colors. Some of them made a habit of living around the water and others on land and in the trees. For the last sixty million years

birds and mammals have overshadowed all other creatures on the earth. That is why we say we are living in
the Age of Birds and Mammals.

I think the hardest thing to understand about this
story of the origin of birds is the tremendous amount of
time it all took. Compared with it, the life we know is
about like the single period at the very end of a good-
sized book. Nobody could possibly have lived long
enough to notice even the smallest changes taking place,
but they were on their way just the same. In fact,
changes are still going on, not only among birds, but
also in mammals, plants and everything else that lives.

Watch Your Step!

You might easily think that a bird's life is a sort of
endless vacation with one good time following another.
Certainly that's the way it looks to most people. But as
soon as you start watching birds, you will notice signs
that make you wonder. Is their life really all fun? Then
you will discover that a bird watches its step carefully
every minute of the day. Otherwise it is likely to get
into very, very serious trouble.

For example, watch the sparrows and chickadees as

Birds are constantly watching for possible danger.

Nuthatch

Song sparrows

White crowned sparrow

they eat seeds and suet at your feeding station. They seem to be thinking of nothing except filling their stomachs. But look more closely. Their eyes keep darting this way and that. Their wings and tails twitch in a nervous manner. Everything shows they are always uneasy. Then suddenly they all whirl away into the nearby bushes, apparently for no reason at all.

They behave this way because they're on guard to escape sudden danger such as a hungry cat, hawk or some other creature that might sneak up and grab them. Usually there is no such peril around. So the birds can come back to their meal after a minute or so. But a small feathered fellow can never be sure, and it's a whole lot better to be safe than sorry. Even a flock of strong pigeons, sunning themselves on a roof, keep cocking their eyes at the sky to make sure there isn't a hawk up there.

Someday a hawk really will come along while you are watching a number of small birds. Every one will disappear in a flash. Most of them dive into thickets, trees, tangled grass or some other nearby spots that will hide them. But now and then one bird will just squat motionless wherever he happens to be, hoping that he won't be noticed. Only very strong and swift fliers, like starlings, are likely to take off into the open where they can make a straightaway race of it.

Woodpeckers have a funny way of hiding if they catch sight of anything they think may be dangerous. Instead of flying, they simply duck around to the other side of the trunk or limb on which they happen to be and cling there without moving a feather. If the enemy should start after them, they may play a regular game of hide-and-seek. They dodge first one way and then the other but always keep the branch between them and the pursuer. And they win this deadly game almost every time.

There's another way in which birds play it safe, too.

Do you remember those photographs of soldiers sneaking through the jungle in queer-looking coveralls spotted with different colors? Have you seen pictures of warships with great curving streaks of green or yellow painted on their sides and smokestacks? Everybody knows that these camouflage markings are to keep the enemy from seeing the soldiers or the warships. But most people do not understand why such tricks work so well. They don't realize that when we use them we are simply copying a plan that most birds and many other wild creatures have followed for millions of years. Naturalists call it "protective coloration."

Good camouflage depends upon three general rules:

1. Strong light makes a dark color seem lighter and weak light causes a light color to look darker.

2. Large areas of any single color are less noticeable if they are broken up here and there by other colors.

3. Any object seems to disappear if it is colored like the background against which you see it.

Since the strongest outdoor light comes from the sky, Rule One explains why so many of the birds, fish, mammals and other wild creatures are paler underneath than on top. If this coloring plan were reversed, they would be far easier to see.

The working of Rule Two can be seen by comparing an all-black crow and a many-colored tropical parrot or toucan. You can spot and identify the crow twice as far away as you can the parrot. One reason for this is that any solid, overall color brings out the *entire outline* of an object, while speckled colors help to hide it. That's why those camouflaged warships are painted with streaks and blotches.

Now for Rule Three. This one is especially important to such birds as sparrows, bobwhites and many pheasants that spend much of their time on or near the ground.

His coloring helps conceal the bobwhite in dry leaves and grass.

Their enemies are most likely to approach them from the side or above. So their wings, backs and sides are often colored and marked in a way that imitates the bits of dead leaves, grass and twigs which so often cover the ground. Frequently such a bird crouches on the ground and stays perfectly still. It matches the background so well that you can scarcely see it even when it is near by. That is also what happens when soldiers wear blotched green and yellow uniforms in the jungle. And ski troops dressed entirely in white are scarcely visible against the mountain snow around them.

Not all birds are protectively colored, of course. For instance, the pure white egret, the bright pink flamingo, and that black crow we spoke of. But in every such case you will find one of two conditions that make up for the lack of camouflage. First, the bird is very wary. It counts on keeping out of danger rather than hiding from it. Or, second, it lives in a region where it has few natural enemies. A bird knows instinctively whether it can be seen easily or not, and usually it acts accordingly.

Nearly all of the really brilliant birds are found where there are plenty of leaves and often flowers on the trees

The coloring of the goldfinch changes with the seasons.

and bushes. Their special kind of camouflage works best in such places. Many of them never leave the leafy tropical jungles. Those that do come north wait until spring when our own flowers and leaves begin to appear. Then, in the late summer or early fall, before the leaves drop from the branches, they hurry back to the South. Scarlet tanagers, orioles, indigo buntings, rosebreasted grosbeaks and quite a number of the warblers are the gorgeous ones you are most likely to see in different parts of the United States in the spring and summer. In none of them does one solid color cover the entire bird.

Our common goldfinch is an amazing example of protective coloration in birds. You probably know that it spends the cold as well as the warm months in the

North. In the spring and summer, the male is brilliant yellow and black. But before the leaves begin to drop in September, his yellow changes to dull green. And by the time the branches are bare, he is almost as quietly colored as a sparrow. You might think he knew enough to change his clothes because the trees were losing their leaves and could no longer hide him. But he doesn't really know or care a thing about that. He's simply doing what every member of the goldfinch family has done for thousands and thousands of years.

The Wonders of a Feather

The whole principle of bird camouflage depends upon the feathers. In fact, there is nothing more truly wonderful than the way a bird's feathers grow from tiny, tiny specks into some of the lightest, strongest and most beautiful objects in the world. Few people have the least idea how feathers do this, or how perfectly they serve the purposes for which they are intended.

Each feather starts in a very small pit or hollow in the inner layer of skin, fitted with a tiny artery and vein. Even before the young bird breaks out of its eggshell, a group of cells begins to grow toward the outside of the skin. When they reach it, they break through, separate, and harden into those shreds of fuzz that you see on most young birds as soon as they dry off after hatching.

Bits of fuzz appear as the newly-hatched bird dries off.

This soft down is not like real feathers, but for a little while it works very well as a covering. Meantime important changes are going on down in those pits, as different sets of cells start making the true or "contour" feathers. Each of these will have a central quill of its own. Pretty soon the tips of these new baby feathers push out into the open air, shoving the shreds of down ahead of them. Each baby feather is rolled tight inside a sort of skin. This keeps the feather so thin and pointed that we call it a pinfeather.

When a young bird has been out of its shell for a week or so, nearly all its true feathers have appeared. Perhaps there are as many as three or four thousand of them in dozens of different sizes, shapes and colors.

But every feather still has a lot of growing to do, and that requires a supply of food. This food is in the bird's blood, which is brought into the pit by that tiny vein and artery. As the feather gets longer and broader, the special artery and vein carrying the blood stay right with it. Gradually they reach out farther and farther within the protection of the strong center quill. In this way the food that the feather needs is always ready for use. Because food from the blood is at work every minute, the feather grows bigger and prettier.

Finally it is fully grown. But it can't keep on growing or it will become too big to fit the bird. So deep down in that little pit where the whole thing started, the artery

Tiny pinfeathers begin to show as the little bird grows up.

and vein are sealed up. Then no more blood can get through. The feather stops growing and dies. But its quill stays stiff, springy and tightly anchored in its socket down in the skin.

Months later, when the feather has become so worn that it loses some of its usefulness, it simply drops out. And immediately those same little cells in the underskin start making another one. The new feather may be a bit different from the one it replaces. This is because some changes in the feather's colors or markings usually take place when a bird grows up. Or changes may occur when the bird shifts from summer to winter plumage and back again the following spring.

It is one thing to read about happenings like these, and another to see some of them with your own eyes. And you can do that very easily.

The next time there is a plucked chicken, turkey or duck ready to go into your kitchen oven, examine it closely. You will find many little bumps on its skin. They are somewhat like pimples with small hollows in the center. Underneath those hollows are the pits from which the feathers grew. Probably in some of them you will find either the stumps of old feathers or the tips of new pinfeathers sticking out. They are scattered more

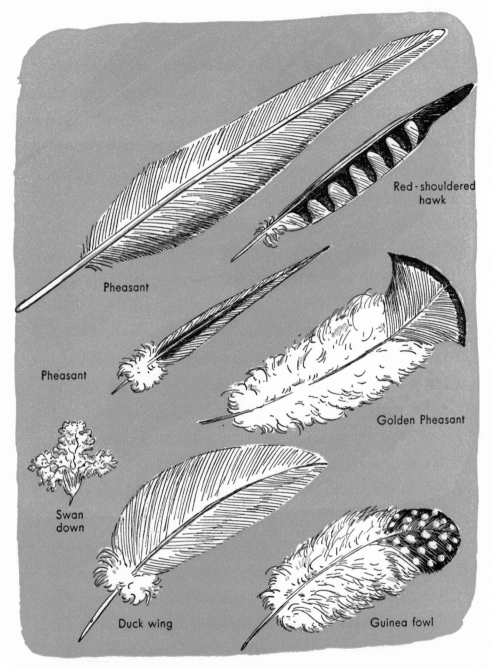

Red-shouldered hawk

Pheasant

Pheasant

Golden Pheasant

Swan down

Duck wing

Guinea fowl

There are bird feathers of many shapes, sizes and types.

or less over the whole body. But they show most thickly on the wings, neck, tail, and in two broad strips down each side of the breast. The pits along the back edges of the wings, and around the stump of the tail, are the biggest. That is because they held the largest feathers with the thickest quills.

When you come across a small pinfeather on the bird you're examining, you will see the thin skin or sheath inside which it is rolled. Slit this lengthwise with a razor blade, and you will find the beginnings of the feather itself. You will also find a dark reddish liquid that is really thick blood. This is the stuff out of which the full-grown feather would be made, right down to its finished tip.

Almost any summer day, you can find on the ground one of those large wing feathers with the thick quills. If you take it home to study, you will find more surprises.

First, press the tip of your finger against the middle of the broad feathery web, or vane, that runs along one side of the quill or shaft. It will stretch almost like thin sheet rubber. When you take your finger away, it will snap back into position. But when you press a little harder, the vane suddenly splits on a long slant. You

Through a magnifying glass a feather shows rows of tiny hooks.

may be able to repair the damage by taking the two sides of the split between your thumb and finger close to the quill and stroking them together along the grain and toward the outer edge of the vane. Suddenly, as you continue this gentle rubbing, the two sides will join and the feather will be as good as ever.

Yes, it is puzzling, but you can understand it by making another split and looking at its edges through a strong magnifying glass. Then you will see that each side of every strand in the vane has a row of hundreds of tiny hooks. When you rub the right way, they lock into the row on the next strand. It's a little like closing the zipper in the front of a windbreaker.

There's a reason for this hook arrangement.

A live bird's wing and tail feathers get pretty hard use. Often this splits their vanes and causes loss of power by letting the air through. A quick and perfect repair is needed. The bird can make one in a jiffy by "zipping" the break together with its bill, as you did with your fingers.

While you are examining the big flight feather, you may be surprised by the hardness and strength of its quill. Yet the whole feather is so light that you can't feel it as it lies across your palm. When you split open the lower part of the quill, you will find it filled with a network of very tough fibers. They are thinner than tissue paper and are separated only by air. This is about the most perfect featherweight bracing arrangement in the world. Out toward the tip, where the shaft is very thin, these fibers become a sort of pith. This is better than a framework for a small space.

It does not seem possible that all this whitish bracing was made from sticky-looking blood carried toward the end of the quill while it was growing. But that is exactly what happened.

There's so much to be learned about feathers and there are so many different kinds that collecting them makes an exciting hobby. You can collect different sizes, shapes, colors and types, and then note their many differences.

For a bird's feathers are a wonderful invention. A bird simply could not live without them, for they make it possible for him to fly.

Flying Secrets

When you watch a bird flying, you will notice that both its wings, even though they may curve backward, work together and seem to be flapping straight up and down. They don't push out behind, the way the oar blades do when you row a boat. If they did, it would be easy to understand why the bird moves ahead so fast. But as those wings flap up and down, you wonder what makes a flying bird go forward.

The real fact is that the wings do move ahead on every down stroke. They pull the rest of the bird along with them. This happens so fast that nobody can see it. The propellers of a plane drag it through the air in the same sort of way, although of course they spin instead of flap. Indeed, it was through studying bird flight that

The downward beat of a bird's wings sends it forward or upward.

men got the ideas for making an airplane that would really work.

When a bird is flying straight ahead, the inner halves of its wings do the same job as those of a plane. That is, they support it while it glides through the air. The outer halves, with their longer, stronger feathers, are the propellers. These are called the big flight feathers or the primary feathers. They are quite stiff but very springy. On the down stroke each one is twisted by the air pressure until it is shaped very much like a propeller blade. This twist pushes backward against the air so hard that the wings move ahead. Of course the whole bird moves too. You might call this downward beat the power stroke, for it is the one that sends the bird in the direction it wants to go.

Now let's look at the upward or "recovery" stroke.

On the upward beat the feathers separate to let air through.

The real purpose of this is to raise both wings into position to start the next downward beat. But it must be done without slowing the bird's forward speed or losing altitude. So, to make it easier, the thin side webs or vanes of the feathers separate from each other. This lets the air slip through so the wings can move up. On the downward or power stroke, the vanes overlap to make a solid sheet that pushes against the air. This explains why it is so important that the thousands of fibers in the vanes can be "zipped" together.

When you have an opportunity to examine any bird's wings, maybe a duck's or even a chicken's, notice how wonderfully the feathers are arranged to do just these things. They even overlap each other from front to back. Thus the whole surface stays smooth as the wings move forward through the air. Every bit of this arrangement has its purpose, and the whole plan is used by every kind of bird that flies.

Of course, birds' wings do many things besides pulling their owners straight ahead. For instance, a longer and stronger power stroke with the right wing than with the left one helps to steer a bird to the left. This is just the way a boat changes its course when you pull very hard on one oar. When it wants to slow down or stop, a flying bird can use its wings as a brake, too. One way it does this is to make its power strokes forward instead of down, something like backing water with oars or a paddle. Another trick is to turn its shorter wing feathers down toward the ground, as a pilot does when he drops the flaps of his plane's wings.

Many birds, such as hawks, eagles, pelicans, and even crows and starlings, can turn themselves into such perfect gliders that they sail for long distances without making a single wing beat. You will see this any day when you're out looking for birds. Also you will soon learn that certain kinds of birds do it much more often than others.

All these flying stunts would be impossible without the right kind of muscles to operate the wings. If you examine the under side of a bird's wing, you will see

The wild duck uses its wings as a brake to slow down for landing.

for yourself the different kinds of bones, muscles, joints and tough, stringy tendons that make it work.

First, there are the long, rather thin muscles that connect the three sets of bones which are the foundation of the whole wing. Out near the tip is the "hand" section, from which the long flight feathers grow. Then comes the "wrist" joint which connects the "hand" and the "forearm." At the inner end of the "forearm" is another larger joint, the "elbow." And finally, you will see the "upper arm" which is joined to the body by a "shoulder" joint that you can hardly find because of the thick muscles which cover it. This whole arrangement of bones and joints is very much like your own arm, and it can be bent, straightened, twisted and turned in much

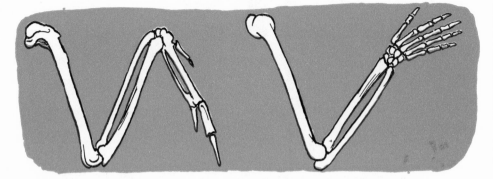

The skeleton of a bird's wing (left) resembles that of a
person's arm (right).

the same way that you bend or twist yours.

But how can a flying bird flap its wings so fast and
for such a long time without a minute's rest?

It will help you understand a bird's muscles if you
test your own. Stretch your right arm straight out to
the side, level with your shoulder. Put the palm of that
hand against the frame of a door or the end of a wall.
Now press your left hand on the upper right part of
your chest. As you give a hard push forward with your
right hand, you will feel those breast muscles tighten.
That is exactly what happens when a bird makes a
downward power stroke with its wings. They push
against the air instead of something solid, as your hand
did.

You will notice that the bird's breast muscles are

many times larger and stronger for its size than any person's. That is why they can keep working hard for a much longer time without getting tired. The entire breast of a bird is chiefly power muscles anchored to each side of the narrow or "keeled" breast bone. You can see this any time you watch a duck or chicken being carved for the dinner table.

A bird's perfect flight is helped by its tail, too, in many different ways. For one thing, the tail feathers can be closed or spread out like a fan as easily and quickly as you close or spread your fingers. Also, the whole tail can be twisted, turned up, down or sideways in an instant, like your hand. In this way the tail helps in mak-

A bird can use its tail to help in making turns and stops.

ing turns, stops and even for straightaway flight. It acts like a plane's rudder, flaps and stabilizer fins. And in the case of long-tailed birds, tails give more supporting surface on which their owners can slip along through the air.

The light weight of birds is another characteristic that helps them fly easily. Even a fair-sized bird like a robin weighs only a few ounces. This is largely because there are air passages and pockets in all parts of its body. They are all connected with the lungs, and all the air comes

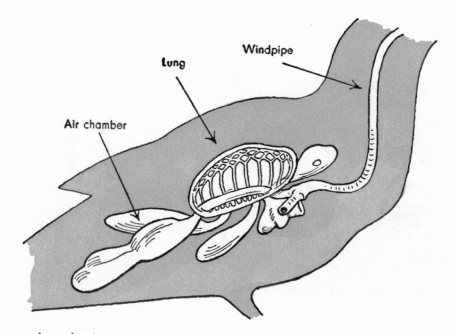

In a bird's body there are many air passages and pockets.

and goes through the mouth and nostrils the way yours does. You might not suspect it, but a bird's body is more thoroughly loaded with air, in proportion to its size, than that of any other animal!

How Fast and How High?

Do you ever wonder what speed a bird is making when it flies past you like an arrow shot from a bow? If it is one of the smaller kinds, such as a sparrow or a woodpecker, it is probably traveling at fifteen to twenty-five miles an hour. But if a hawk should be chasing it, or it is thoroughly scared by something else, its speed may be almost doubled for a short distance. Some of the big, strong birds, especially ducks and geese, can cruise along steadily at a forty- or fifty-mile speed without even getting winded.

No one can be sure which bird flies the fastest, for it is difficult to time a flying bird exactly. However, the record is probably held by either the peregrine (duck hawk) or one of the swift family. Perhaps it is held by the little blackish chimney swift which you see flickering around in the sky on almost any summer day. On the level, peregrines can easily fly at fifty or sixty miles an hour. They have been timed at 180 miles per hour during one of their power dives after another bird. If a swift can go faster than that, he must be a real speed demon!

Altitude flying records are even harder to figure than rates of speed. That is because birds are often so high in the air that you can't see them at all without a good field glass. Mr. Frederick C. Lincoln, who has made a special study of bird travels, says that storks and cranes have been seen flying over the Himalaya Mountains at a height of twenty thousand feet above sea level. This seems to be an unusual case, though, for aviators report that they seldom see birds more than five thousand feet from the ground. As you would expect, the highest fliers are those with the biggest wings compared with the size and weight of their bodies.

As far as we know, the wandering albatross, which looks somewhat like a gigantic gull, has the longest wings. One of these huge ocean birds is known to have measured a little over eleven feet from tip to tip of its fully spread wings.

There seem to be two runners-up for this wing-spread championship. One is the South American con-

The wingspread of an albatross may be over eleven feet.

dor, with at least one record of ten feet. The other is our North American trumpeter swan whose record is ten feet, two inches. It happens, just by chance, that the first of these great birds is mostly black, and the second is entirely white except for a black bill and dark legs.

Not very much is known about how fast different kinds of birds can fly if they really have to. With some luck, though, you may have a chance to find out by keeping your eyes open and doing a little figuring.

For example, when you are traveling in a car you

may see a bird flying in the same direction. It may be near enough for you to estimate its speed by checking it with your speedometer. Train trips, too, often give you chances of the same sort. Here you may have to ask the conductor or one of the brakemen to make sure how fast the train is rolling. And if you go anywhere by plane, remember that pilots have supplied some of the best information we have about the flying speeds of birds and the heights at which they travel. They do it by comparing them with the readings on the plane's instrument dials. To be sure, you won't be sitting in the pilot's seat yourself, but you can see a lot of what is happening by watching through the cabin window.

Not all bird speed records are made in the air. A cock

The ring-necked pheasant can run at tremendous speed.

pheasant can run so fast that you'd really have to hurry to keep up with him. The queer looking road runner found in our southwest desert country is even speedier. I think it is pretty well settled that the champion runner among birds is the ostrich. By taking steps more than twenty feet long, it can trot at fifty miles an hour.

Little Bird That Flies Backward

It has always seemed to me that hummingbirds are the best named of all birds. When they fly, their wings move so fast that they hum as loudly as those of any fly or bee. Actually they often make fifty or sixty strokes a second, sometimes as many as two hundred. You can't even see that they are wings except when they are folded while their owner perches on a twig or the rim of its nest. The rest of the time they buzz so fast that they are just a blur.

There are nearly four hundred full species of "hummers," as many ornithologists call them. All of these are found only on our side of the Atlantic Ocean. Most kinds live in Mexico, Central America and northern South America. A few come north into the United States for the spring and summer. There are about fifteen kinds of hummingbirds in the Far West, and one in the states from the Great Plains to the Atlantic and northward into Canada. This last species is the ruby-throated hummingbird, a good sample of the whole tribe.

The ruby-throat is a little over three inches long from the tip of its needle-like bill to the end of its stubby tail. It weighs only a small fraction of an ounce. Yet it can shoot ahead at fifty or sixty miles an hour. It can fly sideways, backwards or straight up or down as easily as it does forward. It can even hover in the same place as long as it wants to. Surprisingly this tiny creature is a terrific fighter, too. By buzzing around and jabbing with its long, sharp bill, it can drive a crow or some other big bird out of the neighborhood. I never heard of a hawk, cat or any other creature catching a hummer. This midget bird is such a marvelous dodger that grabbing it would be a great deal harder than putting your finger on a flea.

How can anything so small do so many astonishing things?

In the first place, hummer wings are long and narrow, and their feathers are unusually stiff. This means that they can be driven through the air at tremendous speed

As it hunts for food, the hummingbird seems to stop in mid air.

without breaking. Also, the breast muscles which work them are much bigger in proportion to the size of the bird than those of any other species. The whole arrangement makes me think of having a high-horsepower motor in a little rowboat.

When it comes to flying backward, or in any other surprising way it wishes, a hummer simply twists its wings so that the front or "lead" edges face in the direction it wants to go. This keeps the air pressure from getting under the feathers and pushing them out of place because, as you know, each feather on a bird overlaps the one behind it, like the shingles on a roof. The result is that the whole surface stays smooth and streamlined.

All About Birds

As you watch a hummingbird feeding among the garden flowers, you will see all these amazing flying tricks at work, perhaps only a few feet from you. You will notice, too, how the bird pokes its bill deep into blossom after blossom. It seems to stand still in mid air for a moment in front of each one before moving on to the next. It's getting food, of course, but what kind and how?

The answers to these questions are really surprising. The hummer is after the sweet liquid, or nectar, which it finds far inside many kinds of flowers. Lilies, delphiniums, columbine, honeysuckle and salvia are special favorites. Very tiny insects go after this nectar, too, so the hummingbird often gets some of them mixed in with its drink.

The queerest part is how the mixture gets to his stomach. You would naturally think that hummers stick the tips of their bills into this watery food and then swallow —just like that. But these singular little feathered helicopters have a much better system. For their tongues, although hardly thicker than threads, are hollow and can be shot out beyond the ends of their bills. So each hummingbird just puts the end of its bill near the nectar in the flower. Then it sticks out its hollow tongue, probably turns on a tiny suction gadget in its throat, and pulls in the food through the tongue.

If you set up a hummingbird feeder, you may be able to watch this tongue-feeding right in your own door-yard. First, get a little clear glass bottle, and paint the neck of it bright red to catch the hummer's attention. Then twist a piece of wire around it so it can be hung right-side up a few inches from the top of a stake set in the ground among the garden flowers. Next, fill the bottle with a syrup made by dissolving one spoonful of sugar in three spoonfuls of water. Hang it on the stick in full sunlight where you can see it clearly. Then sit down a few yards away and wait quietly.

If you are fairly lucky, a hummer will find this ready-made meal and start drinking. Watch very closely now, and you'll see the bird's tongue flash in and out of the syrup so fast that it actually flickers. Each time it goes down into the bottle a little of the liquid enters its hollow tip. Every time it pulls back and then shoots forward again that small drop moves closer to the bird's throat. So, by darting its tongue out and back dozens of times, the hummer picks up enough of the sweet mixture to satisfy it.

The ruby-throat and many other hummingbirds also

catch small insects on the wing. They like spider eggs and young spiders, too, which they find hiding in the cracks of tree bark and other sheltered places. Sometimes you will see a hummer buzzing close to the trunk of a rough-barked tree, or even an outside wooden shutter on the house. You can be pretty sure, then, that it is on the trail of a spider dinner.

A hummingbird thinks nothing of shooting downward at high speed, for it can pull out of such a power dive without the least danger of crashing. It never takes a chance on doing this over water, however, for it's a dry-land bird first, last and all the time.

High-Dive Champions

The most perfect high-diving exhibition I ever saw was not put on by some member of the Olympic swimming team, but by birds. It took place in August a few years ago. Several of us were in a fisherman's boat a hundred yards or so from the great rock cliffs of Bonaventure Island in the Province of Quebec, Canada. Many thousands of gannets nest on those rocks, and we were there to study them and their family life.

As the boat lay rolling in the long, cold swells of the

North Atlantic, scores of these powerful sea birds were crisscrossing the blue sky above us. Their white bodies and black-tipped wings gleamed in the sunlight. We estimated that each was about three feet long and had a wingspread twice that size. Now and then, one would turn its head to stare down at us. Then its long, sharp-pointed yellow bill looked like the blade of a big dagger hanging over us.

Suddenly one bird, out to seaward from us and per-haps fifty feet above the water, seemed to make a jack-knife dive. It half closed its wings and shot almost straight down. In an instant it was going like a bullet. You'd have felt sure it would be killed unless it pulled out of that terrific dive before it hit the water. But it never wavered. While we held our breath, it disappeared below the surface at a speed that sent a burst of spray ten feet into the air.

Another and another gannet followed suit, until the air seemed full of plunging white bombs and fountains of water. One of them struck so close to us that we could follow its course far into the depths by a swift white trail of bubbles.

All these birds were diving for fish, not for fun. Most of them were starting from a height of forty feet or so.

43

The gannet may dive straight down from a height of fifty feet.

That was because, on that particular day, the fish were swimming so deep that the gannets needed top speed to get below them. Then they would turn and catch their prey on the way up. When the fish are closer to the surface, the dives are not nearly so high and steep. James Fisher, a famous authority on sea birds, believes that gannets probably do not go more than sixty feet under water, even by swimming with their big webbed feet and perhaps with their wings, too. But that's quite a record!

If you had been watching that show with us, you

would surely have wondered why not a single gannet was hurt by hitting the water at such a speed. Most ordinary birds would have been killed on the spot, but gannets are something very special. You see, they always dive headfirst with their big bills pointed straight forward. This splits a hole in the water, the way your hands and arms do when you dive. Also a gannet has special equipment to soften the smash against the water. Under the feathers and skin on a gannet's breast and stomach there are layers of air sacks which act like a pneumatic cushion. No wonder the gannet can survive such a dive!

Almost as daring as the gannets are those big brown pelicans which are so common along the coast of Florida. They're larger, too, and they hit the water with a terrific *wham*. Like the gannets, they lead with their enormous bills, and they have the same sort of built-in air cushions to protect them. But they don't go as far beneath the surface. Both pelicans and gannets close their wings backward and tight against their sides just before they hit. This keeps them from being broken or ripped off. Any time you're in Florida you are sure to see plenty of pelicans diving. There they are so tame that it is easy to get a good look at them. Gannets fly as far south as Florida in the winter, too, but usually they stay so far offshore that it's hard to see them even with a good binocular. The last time I was in Florida, there were a couple of tamed ones at the famous Marineland aquarium on the east coast. If you are ever in that part of the state, you might look them up.

Gannets and pelicans are America's most famous high divers. But a near-champion is often seen along the coast

The osprey grabs a fish in its powerful talons and flies off.

and around inland lakes and big rivers all over the United States and Canada, particularly in summer. He is the osprey, or fish hawk. This high diver is a big fellow, sometimes measuring six feet from one wing tip to the other.

The osprey's method of hunting is to fly fifty feet or more above the water until he spots a good fish fairly near the surface. Then he stops, flutters for a moment, closes his wings and heads for his prey like an express train. Sometimes he gets hurt when he strikes the water with a great splash, but generally there is no damage. He doesn't grab the fish with his bill, as gannets and pelicans do. Instead, he grips it in those powerful curved talons of his, and carries it away to be eaten somewhere along the shore.

It's a Duck's Life

Swimming may be a fine warm-weather sport for people, but to a wild duck it is just an everyday way of making a living right through the year. Ducks must swim in the middle of winter as often as on a hot summer day, for they get nearly all their food from the water or very close to it. They'd starve to death if they didn't go right in after it. So that's what they do and, thanks to some very special equipment, they never get cold or even wet. In fact, they can actually sleep in the water!

If a robin or any other dry-land bird were to jump into deep water, its feathers would be soaked. You have seen what happens when one splatters around in a bird bath. But a duck's feathers are perfectly waterproofed with natural oil. In fact, if you hold one of them under cold water for half an hour it will come out as dry as ever.

A little of this oil is built into the feathers, and some more of it comes from the fat in the skin from which they grow. A lot of it, though, is spread on the plumage from little glands or pockets on the bird's back about where the tail joins the body. These "oil-cans" have outside openings through which the duck can get some of the oil on its bill and then rub it on the feathers needing it most. When you see ducks standing on shore preening their feathers and reaching around to their tails every few minutes, you can be pretty sure that they are putting on fresh waterproofing.

The thickness and strength of a duck's plumage help to keep the bird dry and warm, too. Its body feathers are stiffer than those of most land birds. Also, there are

When ducks preen their feathers, they are really putting on oil.

so many of them and they overlap so perfectly, that they make an amazingly thick, firm blanket.

Furthermore, this oily overcoat has a splendid lining made of the long, beautifully soft down which covers the lower part of each feather's quill. Besides this, the skin itself has still another layer of short fuzz far softer than a mouse's fur. When you work your fingers down into this fluffy, hidden lining, you quickly feel how snug and warm it is. It is like the fleece liner of a good glove.

These three protections from water and cold—the oil, the thickness of the body feathers, and the downy blanket under them—are backed up by a thick layer of yellow fat between a duck's skin and its muscles. Low temperatures have a hard time getting through fat. This is the reason why Channel swimmers cover themselves with grease before taking off, and why fat people generally shiver less than thin ones on a chilly day. The fatty layer on a duck or goose covers most of its body. It is thickest on the breast and stomach because those are the parts which are in the water most of the time.

It takes a lot of food to keep such a big, heavy bird going in every sort of weather. As a result all ducks have terrific appetites.

There are more than thirty species of ducks in this country. These are divided into two general classes: those that dive below the surface to get their meals, and those that don't. The divers eat such things as fish, parts of water plants, and little shellfish. When hunting for these, they sometimes swim around under water for a couple of minutes before coming up for air. When they do finally pop out, they catch a few good breaths and then go under again.

Other kinds of ducks, most of which you are likely to see around fresh rather than salt water, hardly ever dive below the surface. Instead, they have a comical way of poking their heads and long necks under water and then paddling with their feet so as to push their tails straight up into the air. Shallow water is the favorite eating place of ducks like these. They love to puddle around with their bills on a muddy bottom and swallow dozens of the little worms and plants and bugs that live there. They are fond of shelled corn, too. Sometimes you can attract a lot of them to a quiet, shallow cove in a lake or river by throwing corn into the water so that it can sink to the bottom.

Mallard ducks often feed with their tails straight up in the air.

Nearly all kinds of ducks build their nests on the ground or maybe on a grass tussock hidden in a marsh. There may be anywhere from six to a dozen eggs. Almost as soon as they hatch, the ducklings start trotting around. By the time they are a day or two old, they can swim like old-timers. They never have to be taught to swim. The very first time they see water they will hop in and paddle away like fuzzy little toy boats.

One of the queerest things about wild ducks is that four species of them—the golden-eye, bufflehead, wood duck and hooded merganser—pay no attention to the family habit of nesting on the ground or in a swamp. Instead, they lay their eggs in old tree holes, maybe as much as fifty feet up in the air. Wood ducks will even use a bird house, if it is big enough and is fastened to a tree near a quiet pond or wooded creek. Occasionally the American merganser, a big cousin of the hooded, tries tree-hole nesting, too.

Perhaps you wonder how the ducklings get down from these hole nests and reach the water where they really belong. Well, if the tree trunk is slanting, they sometimes scramble down it any old way. But if it is straight, they just jump and take their chances. The strange part of it is that they never seem to get hurt, even if they land *splat* on a patch of hard ground or even a rock.

A duck's life is different from any other bird's, and mostly it is a windy, rough and rugged one. But ducks are so well built to stand bad weather that even a heavy storm doesn't seem to ruffle their feathers. This toughness is one of the important reasons why they can make their long migration flights quite easily and safely in weather so wild that it would probably kill many smaller, weaker species.

Why Do Birds Migrate?

Nearly every kind of wild bird in the United States and Canada flies southward in the autumn and back again in the spring. Some species go only fifty or a hundred miles in each direction. Many more travel twenty or thirty times that distance. This great round-trip journey is known as migration. Each species sticks so closely to a traveling schedule that on both trips the first ones often reach their destination within a few days of the same date, year after year.

North American birds have been migrating like this for many thousands of years, and we still do not know exactly why or when they started it. As you can easily see, it is a tremendously important habit that causes many changes in the kinds of birds you see at different times of the year.

One of the chief reasons for bird migration is food. North America has billions of birds. They all have to eat, and it takes tons of food every day simply to keep them alive. That is one reason why they are spread all over the country.

Each species of bird must have plenty of the right kinds of food, particularly when it is raising a young family in the spring and summer. Warblers, tanagers and other insect-eaters that nest in the North find lots of nourishing bugs during the warm weather, but very few in winter. So in late summer or early fall they fly south toward the equator where it's warm and where all sorts of insects are plentiful even in January and February.

Millions of northern-nesting birds do exactly this. You might think that tropical birds would run short of food during the winter because of the crowds of hungry birds from the North. Perhaps they would if the visitors settled down for a long time. But along about February or March, the orioles and the rest of the northern nesters begin their return trip. They keep pace, more or less, with the warm weather as it moves north. Thus they reach their regular breeding grounds by the time the fresh crop of bugs up there is ready to be eaten. Meanwhile, down in the tropics, the stay-at-homes once more have it all to themselves.

This is the way it works out with all the birds that migrate north and south, no matter what they eat. Food supplies in the North vary a lot between summer and winter, and birds always go where they can be sure of finding the particular meals and general conditions they like.

In general, all birds have two principal needs. First, a steady food supply throughout the year. And second, the right kind of surroundings and temperature during the breeding season. Without any of these they'd be in trouble, so migratory birds make sure of having everything by flying back and forth according to the time of year. Other species which stay in the tropics all their lives find all they need right there at home. They migrate very little either north or south.

Nobody is sure when this migration habit began and what started it. Some scientists think it can be explained by studying the effects of the Ice Age.

About a hundred million years ago, all of North America had such a warm climate that birds lived practically anywhere and did not have to go far south to escape the cold. Then, during the Ice Age great ice sheets or glaciers formed and began to creep very slowly southward. Few birds could stand the low temperatures that came along with this ice, so most of them had to crowd together in the warm tropics.

After a long time, the glaciers began to melt away, and the North started warming up again. This gave great numbers of birds a chance to get away from the over-crowded tropics by heading north once more. But what did they find there? Just this: during what we now call spring and summer everything was fine, but in a short time it would turn cold again and they'd have to go back to the South. This invasion by the glaciers was repeated

Scarlet tanager male

Scarlet tanager female

Yellow warbler

The scarlet tanager and yellow warbler are migratory birds.

several times, and the birds always had to give way before it.

The plain fact was that the North American climate was changing into the kind of climate we have today—spring, summer, autumn and finally winter. The only thing the birds could do about it was to get into the habit of flying back and forth, back and forth. Now, after millions of years, they do it naturally.

That is one explanation, and maybe it's the right one. But other scientists think that migration began for different reasons.

They believe that originally all birds lived in the tropics, but after a long time they became so crowded that they had to spread out. Going north in the spring gave a great many of them a chance to raise their families where there was more space and plenty of food, so that's what they did. By the time cold weather drove them back south the other species which had stayed behind had gotten a rest from being so crowded. Thus all could get along until the next spring rolled around.

Either of these ideas about the beginning of migration may be the correct one—or both of them may be wrong! For, you see, it all happened so long ago that there wasn't anybody around to keep records of it. But there is no doubt about this: tremendous numbers of birds *do* migrate, and you can see and hear them doing it right around your own home.

For example, on almost any day in October or November you may sight a flock of robins, blackbirds, ducks or wild geese overhead. They are flying southward for the winter. And, when March and April finally come again, there will be the same flocks, or others like them, heading in exactly the opposite direction. Here is daytime migration right before your eyes, a habit that was already an old story long before the first white people came to America.

Yet this is only a small part of the mystery, for countless thousands of birds, particularly the little ones like warblers and sparrows, migrate under cover of darkness. And you can catch them at it, too.

Some clear, pleasant night in spring or early fall, just stand outdoors in a quiet spot and listen carefully. Pretty soon you will hear a faint chirp high overhead, then another and another. Though you cannot see the birds, you know that those sounds are the calls of small feathered travelers hurrying forward through the dark sky. And if there happens to be a full moon, and you can watch it through a telescope or a strong binocular, you will see little black figures zipping across at surprising speed. They will be too far away for you to be sure what kinds they are. But from their general shape and the rapid beat of their wings you can tell that they're migrating birds and are really on their way!

There are two principal migration routes through the United States. One is fairly close to the Atlantic Coast and the other follows the Mississippi Valley and its upper branches. Ornithologists call the first the Atlantic

The arctic tern may travel as much as 22,000 miles in a year.

Flyway and the other the Mississippi Flyway. And there are always a considerable number of species that fly back and forth between them. This helps to spread the bird population fairly evenly across the whole country, of course.

A great many of the species that migrate east of the Rocky Mountains spend the winter in Central America and the northern parts of South America, even though their summer homes are in Alaska and lower Canada. Great numbers of those which use the Mississippi Flyway cross the Gulf of Mexico to the Yucatan Peninsula from the Texas and Louisiana coasts in autumn and return by the same route in the spring. Some Atlantic Flyway species do the same thing, but many others travel back and forth through Florida and the West Indies. Bobolinks, which breed across the upper half of the country from the Atlantic almost to the Pacific, winter in southern Brazil. They use both of the big flyways.

One of the most remarkable migrants is the golden plover. It is a graceful, long-winged little fellow that raises his family in the arctic. In late summer and early all both old and young take off over the open Atlantic. If they have good weather, many of them don't stop until they reach the northern coast of South America on the way to their winter resort in Argentina and southern Brazil.

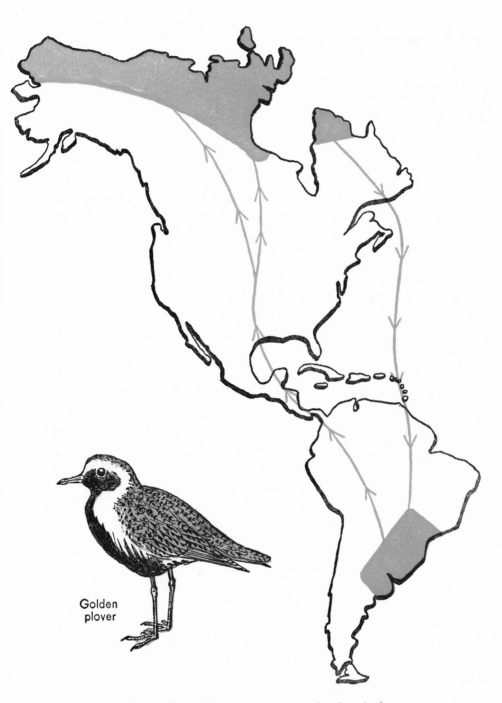

Golden
plover

The graceful little golden plover uses both of the great
flyways from the arctic to South America and back.

All About Birds

Probably the longest migration trip of all is made by the arctic tern, a sea bird which summers in the arctic and winters in the antarctic!

Migration is a risky undertaking for small birds, and many of them lose their lives along the way. One of the greatest dangers arises when several cold, rainy days come along during the spring migration. When that happens, a lot of the warm weather species like warblers and scarlet tanagers are killed. You see, that sort of weather drives small insects into hiding, so that the birds cannot find enough food to keep them going.

And sometimes unexpected storms and heavy fogs develop while birds are migrating at night. These may blow them out to sea, beat them down to the ground, or confuse them so badly that hundreds are killed by banging headfirst into lighthouses and even city skyscrapers. Luckily, such accidents do not happen often.

Favorite Foods

What are the foods which billions of birds fly so far and so dangerously to get? Where do they find them?

The birds' dinner table is really the whole outdoor world. Some of their meals are in every river, lake and ocean, deep in the water or floating on the surface. Other kinds are along the shores and beaches, and still others are in the marshes. Many different kinds of birds go to such places to eat—ducks, gulls and terns in the open water, sandpipers along the shores, and herons in the marshes. They find fish, frogs, water plants, tiny shellfish, and dozens of different kinds of insects. Each sort of bird picks up the particular things it wants. It leaves the rest for some other creature. So all of them are perfectly satisfied.

On dry land most of the food is quite different and attracts different birds. Sparrows, bobwhites, meadowlarks and other ground birds search in the grass and dead leaves for their foods. There they find their favorite weed seeds, insects, grubs and so on. The bushes and smallish trees are perfect food counters for warblers and many others that prefer fruit, caterpillars and various above-ground insects.

Up in the taller trees you will find still other species of birds. They are looking for their special foods found only in such places. And in the open air itself, where only flying creatures can go, you see the flycatchers and swallows. Like the others that catch their meals on the wing, they dart this way and that all day, filling their

The tree sparrow likes nothing better than weed seeds.

hungry stomachs in mid air.

This is the way it goes all over the world wherever there are mountains or oceans, prairies or deserts, ice fields or steaming jungles, or any other sort of place you can think of. Where there is anything for them to eat, there you will find birds. Sometimes there are only a few of them, but often there are many. And all will be hunting out the meals which suit them best. Practically every bird will eat several kinds of food—seeds, beetles and caterpillars, for example. Thus a bird is not likely to go entirely hungry even if it cannot find its favorite food.

There are a number of reasons why birds scatter so

far and wide over the earth for their food. For one thing, if all of them stayed in the same place, they would quickly eat up everything in sight and then die of starvation. And if there were no birds in other parts of the country, the weeds, insects and other live foods in those areas would multiply so fast that they'd use up all *their* food.

This is how it works with every living wild thing on earth. Each one has certain habits. Some of them keep it alive and some help to keep others alive. And so all the different forms of life manage to stay in rather good balance as long as we human beings don't interfere with them.

I suppose that many freight trains would be needed to carry all the food eaten by our billions of North American birds in the course of only a few days. Years ago a well-known scientist calculated that, in the state of Iowa alone, the little tree sparrows that spend the winter there ate at least 875 tons of weed seeds during their annual cold-weather visit. When just one species does that in a single state, think what the hundreds of other kinds spread all over the country must swallow!

There is practically no end to the list of foods that are eaten at some time by some kind of bird. Here are a few of the more important ones:

Mice, rats, squirrels, rabbits, chipmunks, ground moles, snakes, skunks and even birds. These make good meals for hawks and owls, and now and then for a vulture, shrike, eagle or black-backed gull.

Loons, herons, gulls, cormorants, terns, kingfishers, many ducks, a few shore birds, some hawks and strange-looking waders such as the limpkin, choose from among tidbits like small and medium-size salt- and fresh-water fish, frogs, tadpoles, snails, clams, lizards and even worms.

Many kinds of big and little land birds, including those that you see around home, have a long food list

The cedar waxwing prefers a meal of cherries or wild berries.

to choose from. On it you would find all sorts of seeds, young leaves and plant stems, buds, sweet corn, peas, grapes, strawberries, raspberries, cherries, wild berries, acorns, beechnuts, and countless different beetles, cater‑pillars, flies, grubs and other insects of all sizes.

Yes, it all adds up to quite a full list of foods. Nearly every wild bird you see flying or hopping about is after something to put in its stomach. The meals it eats and how it gets them are some of the strangest discoveries which are waiting for you any day right in your own neighborhood.

Big Mouths and Little Ones

Birds' mouths are just about as different from ours as anything could be. They have no teeth and no lips. Their two mandibles, or jaws, stick so far out in front that sometimes they are two or three times as long as the whole head. Besides all this, their bills can pick up things a great deal faster and more nimbly that we could even by using all our fingers.

Most people think that a bird's bill—that hard, bare projection which looks like a sort of nose—is all there is to a bird's mouth. However, this is only part of it. When

67

the upper and lower mandibles are separated, you'll find that the opening between them leads right back into the feathers of the face. That surprising space is a very important part of the true mouth. One queer thing about it is that sometimes its opened size has nothing to do with the length or thickness of what you would call the regular bill or beak.

For example, sparrows and other birds that live mostly on little seeds have short, thick bills and small mouth openings to match. On the other hand a sandpiper, whose bill is very long and thin, has a small mouth opening instead of the large one you would expect. It's the same way with the long-billed hummingbird, whose tiny mouth you have heard about. But a kingfisher with his tremendous bill sometimes grabs a fish that looks big enough to choke him. He is able to eat it because his mouth opens almost as far back as his eyes and, more strangely still, because he swallows his catch headfirst so it won't get jammed across his throat.

The mouths of most of the insect-eaters are bigger than those of the little seed-eaters, for they must be able to manage a good-sized bug if they happen to catch one. But if you want to see mouths that can open up almost like the prow of a landing ship, watch the nighthawks,

The kingfisher devours his catch headfirst.

whip-poor-wills, swifts and swallows. These four types of wing-feeding birds have mouths that are the world's best flying bug traps. They can catch a tremendous amount of food that will give their owners the strength to stay on the wing for hours at a time.

If you look closely, you will see that their mouths are very wide from side to side and open away back below the eyes. You will notice, too, that the forward part of the bill looks much too small for the rest of it.

Some of these large-mouthed fellows catch much of their food in a very special way. Instead of grabbing the bugs in their beaks one at a time, as the strong-billed phoebes and other regular flycatchers do, they often scoop them in by the dozen. When they see a swarm of little insects, they simply open their big mouths wide and swoop right through the crowd, dodging around to find the thickest parts of it. I couldn't make a guess at how many insects can be trapped in a single dive, but it could be a lot. One ornithologist who shot a nighthawk for scientific study found in its stomach 2,175 flying ants which it had caught and not yet digested.

Besides being very large, the mouth of a whip-poor-will has stiff bristles sticking out on each side. These really make the trap still wider. They are especially useful for catching those large night-flying moths of which the birds are very fond. In fact, whip-poor-wills like such food so much that they probably don't bother with the small insects which nighthawks, swifts and swallows gobble up so eagerly.

Some day when you come across a dead bird—any kind of bird—examine it and you will see exactly what I mean by the difference between "bill" and "mouth." You will discover something else very interesting, too. The lower half of the bill is the part that works up and down. But the upper part is so much a part of the skull that it can hardly move in any direction. This is

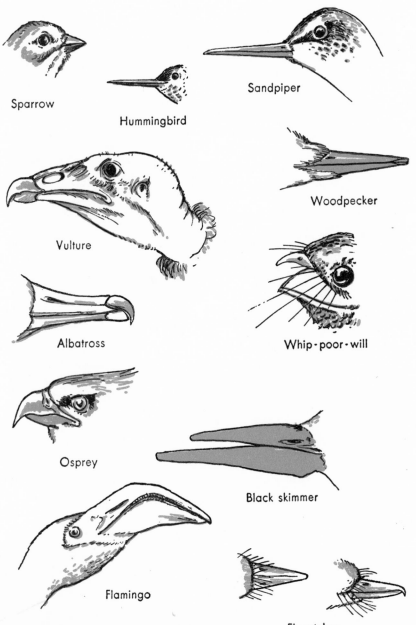

Sparrow

Hummingbird

Sandpiper

Woodpecker

Vulture

Whip-poor-will

Albatross

Osprey

Black skimmer

Flamingo

Flycatcher

Birds have different kinds of mouths and beaks that permit them to eat different kinds of food.

the way your own mouth is built; the lower jaw makes just about all of the chewing movements. Also, the hinge joints of your mouth and a bird's mouth are away back under the ears.

So far as I know, only two kinds of birds have an upper jaw which moves and a lower jaw that doesn't. The first of these is the black skimmer. It is a big black-and-white sea bird that feeds by flying along just above the water and "skimming" or "plowing" the surface with its very long, strong lower mandible. If this were hinged the way a human jaw is, it could easily be thrown out of joint if it happened to dip too deep into the top of a wave. You can imagine how serious that would be.

The skimmer does most of his feeding at night. As he skims the water, the disturbance causes the tiny phosphorescent creatures in the water to glow. Their light attracts many little fish. Then the skimmer turns around and flies back along the wet track he has just made and scoops up the unsuspecting fish.

The second bird with a motionless lower mandible is the flamingo, a strange fellow if ever there was one. He has tremendously long legs and neck and a big, thick, curved bill. When he feeds, he sticks his head into the

The flamingo sticks his head in the water so the top of his bill is on the bottom.

water until the top of his bill is on the bottom. Then he chomps away with his movable upper mandible so that it pumps mud and water against the motionless lower one. In this way he strains out the little shellfish and things which are the favorite food of every flamingo.

So, you see, this whole story of big mouths, long bills or short ones, has some real purposes behind it. Like so many other surprising truths about birds, the kinds of mouths they have are an important part of the lives they live and the meals they eat. You can always be sure of this: no matter how strangely a bird may look and act, there is always at least one good reason for it.

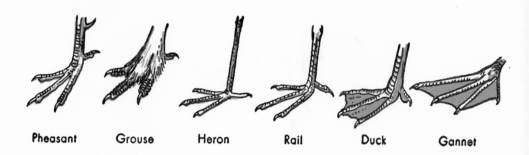

| Pheasant | Grouse | Heron | Rail | Duck | Gannet |

All Kinds of Feet

People everywhere have the same sort of feet and use them for the same purpose: to stand, walk and run on. But the feet of birds have to do all sorts of jobs from paddling around a pond to gripping a branch or catching snakes and rabbits. So there are more kinds and sizes of them than you could imagine. Suppose we examine some of them and see what tales they have to tell of the ways their owners live.

First, there is the walking or "pedestrian" type of foot, like that of a turkey, pheasant, grouse, chicken or any other fowl-like species. The three forward toes of such a bird are strong and fairly long. The rear one is a great deal shorter and grows much higher on the leg. In some cases, its nail or claw hardly touches the ground. This makes a perfect foot for walking or running on dry ground, or scratching among dead leaves and grass to

74

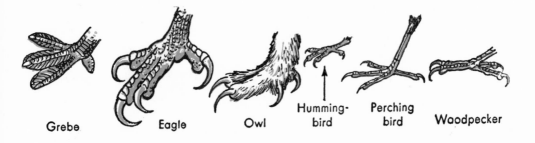

Grebe   Eagle   Owl   Humming- Perching   Woodpecker
                                 bird   bird

uncover seeds, bugs or other food. Work like this is pretty rough, and so all the toenails are short and stout. Even the legs are very strong and able to carry the bird's heavy body around for a long time without getting tired.

Rails and herons need very different feet. These queer-looking birds spend much of their time in marshes and other wet places. Their toes are unusually long in order to keep them from sinking too far into the mud. Often there is plenty of dead grass and weed stems lying on the bottom. At every step the birds' slim, widely spread toes are able to step on so many pieces of this that they don't go down very deep. It's rather like the way skis or snowshoes hold you up in soft snow.

Of course, the feet of real swimming birds, such as gulls, ducks and geese, have broad webs which turn them into perfect paddles. In most cases the web is made of tough, leathery skin which connects the three forward toes. It would be hard to hitch up a hind toe in such an arrangement, and so a duck has only a very small one. But gannets, cormorants and pelicans have back toes that grow out to one side where a web joins them with the shortest front toe. This increases the paddling area nearly one-third.

When one of these web-footed birds makes a backward or "power" swimming stroke, it spreads its toes so as to stretch out the web. This makes as large a surface as possible with which to push against the water. But on the "recovery" stroke, the toes are pulled together and bent toward the rear. Then the web folds up. As the leg sweeps forward, the whole foot slips through the water easily and without slowing down the bird's speed.

A few of the swimming water birds, especially the coots, do not have regularly webbed feet. Instead, each toe has two or three pairs of little flaps. These work almost like hinges, opening to catch the water on the power stroke and closing on the recovery. The grebes, which some people call "hell-divers," have paddles that are halfway between flaps and full-size webs.

For a very different kind of foot, look at that of a bird of prey like an eagle, hawk or owl. All these fellows eat live, active creatures such as squirrels, mice, rats, frogs, snakes and even birds. They catch them *with their feet*. No wonder they need those thick, very powerful toes, all four of them tipped with long, hooked and very sharp nails. The largest of these flesh-eating birds have a very strong grip. If one of them really grabbed a heavy leather hunting boot, it could drive its

The bald eagle catches its prey with thick, powerful toes.

meat hooks right through and into the foot inside. I once had a wounded South American eagle do that to my foot, so I know what it feels like!

A hummingbird has feet as different from those of a hawk as night is from day. Of course, a hummer is awfully small, but even so its feet seem too little to be of any use at all. These tiny feet couldn't possibly walk a step. About the only thing they ever do is to cling to some support, like a twig, when their owner wants to rest a bit.

Why don't hummingbirds have more useful feet? Well, the reason is that hummers do all their feeding on the wing. They really don't need better feet. It's pretty much the same way with the weak-footed swallows, which catch millions of little flies just by flying at them with their mouths open. Once in a while, though, swallows do manage to waddle around on the ground a little as they gather mud for their nest-building.

For generally useful feet that can do almost anything, there's nothing like those of the big group called perching birds — sparrows, wrens, blackbirds, warblers, thrushes, flycatchers, chickadees, jays, tanagers, waxwings and some others. All these use their feet in many different ways, from walking to hopping and climbing around among the trees. As you would expect, all four toes are good-sized and fairly long-nailed. They have the nimbleness needed for a quick, sure hold on almost any object from a weed stalk to a limb as thick as your leg.

Most perching birds have gray, brown or blackish feet, though in a few species they are pale and sometimes almost pinkish. But a black duck's paddles are red, a sora rail's feet are green, and those of a hawk and a snowy egret (one of the white herons) are as yellow as dandelions!

The longer you study birds' feet the more remarkable they seem. There is a definite purpose in every little

Hermit thrush

Chickadees

Perching birds have feet that can hold on to almost any object.

detail—the shape of the nails, the number of joints, the size of the scales on the toes and the different ways they overlap. If you find it hard to remember the different kinds we've been talking about, try copying the pictures carefully with a pencil and paper. That's a good way to make them really stick in your mind, and you'll be surprised how well you can draw them after a little practice. You might start with those of the woodpeckers, for these fellows are very special birds, not only in their feet, but in many unexpected ways.

Woodpecker Oddities

It is likely that woodpeckers will be among the first birds you learn to recognize. This is because of their noisiness, their tree-climbing habits and their handsome, generally black-and-white markings. There are twenty-eight different kinds of woodpeckers in this country and Canada. Each one is as full of odd manners and strange devices as the ocean is full of water.

Notice their feet, for one thing. Most birds have three good-sized toes in front and a smaller one behind, but not so with the woodpeckers. Their lives depend so much upon being able to get a good grip on the bark

The woodpecker's long-clawed toes give him a good grip.

of an upright tree that nearly all of them have two long-clawed toes in front and two behind. All four of them are unusually large and strong. Also, the ends of their longest tail feathers are very stiff and sharp-pointed. When climbing a tree trunk with its claws, a woodpecker gets extra support by pressing these special feathers hard against the bark. This is done in such a way that the feather points catch firmly in the bark and make first-rate props. When you watch one, you'll see at once how perfectly this system works.

If it weren't for these special foot- and tail-grips, I don't suppose any woodpecker would be able to chop out the wood the way he does with that chisel-pointed bill of his. He really makes the chips fly as he hacks his way in to the spot where some fat wood borer is hiding. When you see the speed and force of those blows, you might think he'd knock himself out, or at least get a terrific headache. But his skull is thick enough for an ordinary bird several times his size. Probably his brain isn't even jarred when he hits the wood.

Another woodpecker oddity is the tongue. Its tip is hard, sharp and has little barbs something like those on a fish spear. The bird can stick it far out beyond the tip of his bill, too. When he has chopped his way in to the

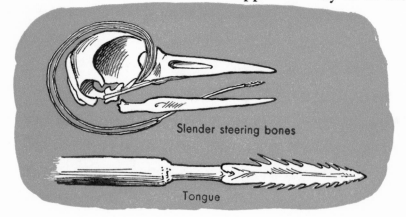

Slender steering bones

Tongue

The tip of the woodpecker's tongue is sharp and barbed.

borer he wants for dinner, he just spears it with his tongue and pulls it back into his mouth. The butt-end of the tongue, by the way, is steered by two very slender, springy bones. Like the arms of the letter Y, they go up over the back of the head and then forward. Because each of these lies in a tiny groove in which it slides back and forth, you might say the two of them keep everything on the track. Hummingbirds have the same sort of arrangement, and it never fails to work perfectly.

How can these hard-headed birds tell the exact position of a borer hidden under perhaps an inch or more of wood? Nobody is really sure about this, but many guesses have been made.

Maybe a woodpecker has such good ears that he can hear his victim chewing or stirring around. Certainly you will see the bird stop chopping and cock his head as if listening. Other people have suggested that the bird may be able to tell, simply by the sound of the wood when he strikes it, whether it is solid or has a small, deep hole in it such as a borer or carpenter ant always makes. Or maybe the wood near where one of these chewers is at work has a slightly different color from the rest of it, which the woodpecker can spot.

All About Birds

For still another explanation, it might be possible that the location is found by the woodpecker's bill being able to feel tiny vibrations from the movements of the grub or whatever it is that he's after. This idea seems to me to be a pretty poor one, because the birds find plenty of food in the middle of winter when all sensible borers are hibernating and not moving a muscle.

As you may know, woodpeckers chop out nest-holes, mostly in dead trees. Here they lay their eggs and bring up their young. But have you ever looked at the inside of one of these neat caves and seen how smooth and well shaped it is? There isn't one scrap of bedding in it except a few small chips left over from the chopping. One of these days you'll come across such a nesting hole in a dead stub in the woods and have a chance to cut it open. Then you will learn what perfect wood carvers its makers really are.

Sometimes a pair of nuthatches or chickadees moves into one of these abandoned nests and raises a family there. The woodpeckers don't mind, for they like to peck out new ones for themselves every spring. Often, too, they go to the trouble of chopping roosting holes just to sleep in at night—a very good idea for cold or stormy weather!

A woodpecker has nothing that we would call a regular song, but the males do make a terrific noise that serves the same purpose. You will hear this sound many times in late winter and early spring. It is a loud, rapid tattoo very much like a short drum roll. This is the bird's "song." He produces it by hammering with his bill on a dead branch. Once he finds a spot that gives the exact tone he wants he will drum on it eagerly day after day. In quiet weather, with little wind, you can easily hear him at a distance of a quarter-mile or more.

When you know the woodpeckers fairly well, you can identify them far away by their habit of flying in a series of dips and rises as if they were on an easy, straightaway roller coaster. You will notice another interesting habit, too. When lighting on a tree trunk woodpeckers always swoop *up* to the spot where they plan to land. By doing this they're sure of being in the right position to start climbing.

However, not all woodpeckers do everything exactly alike. Take the matter of food, for example. It is true that most of them stick pretty closely to a diet of insect grubs. They also eat suet at feeding stations. But downy woodpeckers, one of our smallest and commonest species, sometimes eat berries of poison ivy; redheaded woodpeckers go for small fruits; California woodpeckers make hundreds of little holes in which they store acorns for winter meals. Flickers, which are brown woodpeckers, love cherries, pepperidge berries, and ants which they catch by sticking their tongues down into ant burrows in the ground. And, stranger still, sapsuckers drill rows of small holes in trees and drink the sap which collects in them along with bits of soft inner bark and possibly tiny insects!

Habits They Never Get Over

As you come to know the birds in your neighborhood, you will find that many kinds besides the woodpeckers have special habits by which you can recognize them at quite a long distance. These manners are often a great help in identifying a bird, for every single one of a particular species will act in just about the same way.

Starlings give an example of the kind of thing I mean.

Except during the nesting season, these chunky, blackish birds are almost always in flocks of four or five to several hundred. So are the different species of blackbirds, most of the ducks and geese, and nearly all the sandpipers and plovers that you see along the shores of big lakes, rivers and the ocean beaches. The flocking habit is as much a part of their nature as are their calls and manner of flying.

Heron habits are exactly the opposite of this. These long-necked, long-legged fellows nest in flocks or colonies. But during the rest of the year each one lives pretty much by itself during the daytime. Only in that way can it have good luck in catching the wary fish, frogs and other small creatures on which it feeds. You very seldom see a flock of hawks. They too are almost always lone rangers except when a pair of them is raising a family in the spring. The only hawk I know of that likes a crowd is the broad-winged hawk, which often travels in big, loose flocks when migrating to its winter home in South America.

For a very different sort of habit, you'll find that several kinds of small birds have a funny way of tilting their tails down and then up again every minute or so. One of these is the hermit thrush, and another is the phoebe, perhaps our best known flycatcher. Palm warblers do the same thing. But three other common warblers —the myrtle warbler, the magnolia warbler and the redstart—often spread their tails like fans as if they want to show how pretty they are. And wrens have a way of pointing their tails straight up in the air or even tipping them forward toward their heads!

Wren

Redstart

Some birds can be recognized by the tilt of their tails.

Most of the birds that have crests, such as bluejays, cardinals and cedar waxwings, frequently raise these long feathers so high that you could never mistake them for other species. Why they do this is something of a mystery, but probably it is the result of some sort of excitement. During the mating season, of course, the males show off their handsome crests to make a good impression on the females.

Most birds, as you know, drink by standing at the edge of a pool or some other bit of water and dipping their bills into it. Then they raise their heads so that the water can run down their throats. But you almost never see swallows do that. Instead, they usually drink on the fly, skimming close to the surface of a pond or quiet river and scooping up a few drops with their bills as they go. You can see this strange habit almost any summer day. And when you do, you know that bird is a swallow as far away as you can see it.

Probably one reason for this drinking while on the wing is that swallows' feet and legs are very small and awkward. Moving on the ground to the edge of a pool would be quite a chore. Also, their mouths open so far back of the real bill that drinking in the ordinary bird way might not work too well.

Have you noticed that some kinds of birds walk or

Cardinal

Bluejay

Others can be identified by their handsome crests.

trot the way we do, swinging from one foot to the other? But others hop with both feet together. Pigeons, doves, starlings, sandpipers, quail, pheasants and meadowlarks are some of the true walkers. Sparrows and towhees generally hop. All of these birds have at least fairly good feet and legs. You'd think they would use them any way they felt like. But habits like these were built into them so very long ago that they just cannot be changed. These habits are connected with the kinds of lives birds live, the foods they eat, and where they find those foods.

This explains why kingfishers and practically all kinds of flycatchers spend so much of their time perched on fences, posts, dead branches and other exposed spots—a trait which is often a real aid in identifying them. Such places are perfect lookouts from which to take off after fish or flying insects, as the case may be. Most kinds of hawks have the same sort of habit for the same general reason, and it will help you identify them a long way off.

Crows are as full of interesting habits as any person you ever saw. One of the most entertaining of these is their trick of ganging up on a big hawk, owl or even a fox and raising such a noisy row that usually they drive

A dead tree is a favorite lookout for many kinds of hawks.

him far away. I suppose they're afraid of what might happen if any of these enemies caught one of them. So the first crow that sights the foe yells for reinforcements. Then all the others within hearing come boiling along to help in a mass attack.

These are only a few of the many, many actions and manners that help to make one kind of bird different from other kinds. Once you start looking for these habits, you will be surprised how easy it is to recognize them. You will find it is fun to discover and watch more and more new ones yourself.

The friendly wood thrush is a well-known singer.

Singing in the Spring

After a long, cold winter, the return of pleasant spring weather makes everybody feel better and want to go out and do things like playing baseball, hiking in the woods or visiting the zoo. In the longer, warmer days the whole earth and all living things on it seem to wake up and get busy.

The springtime singing of birds is an important part of this active season. You can tell just by listening to it. The birds' spirits are high, and so they sing like mad. But if you manage to get a good look at one of the singers, you will notice a queer fact. The singer is sure to be a male bird. Almost never will you find a female saying anything except the ordinary chirps and other calls used by all her brothers and sisters.

For many years scientists have studied this strange truth that the males do practically all the singing. Now they believe there are several reasons for it. One is that the bird is in very high spirits because of the long days. For another, he wants to make a good impression on some female of his own kind.

Probably the most important reason of all, however, is that he wants to warn all other males of his species that he has chosen this spot as his own. It may be a garden, a bit of woods, or a brushy field. But it is his domain, for himself and the new family he expects to have. He knows that if the other birds don't keep away there may not be enough food for all. He is saying, in a way, that if trespassers of his own kind come on his property he'll fight them. Of course, he doesn't actually *think* about these things the way we would. He does them just by instinct. It amounts to a habit that has been going on for so many thousands of years that he follows it now without thinking.

Another point to remember is that, in the birds' world, it is the male's job to do most of the fighting. He

defends the home grounds, while his mate builds the
nest, lays the eggs and takes care of them. Because all
the males of any one species sing very much alike, they
can understand each other. So when one of them sings
from more or less the same place day after day, the
others know he is defending that neighborhood.

Most of the singing is done in the spring and the first
half of summer. This is because it is the season for mating, nest building and family raising. When the young
birds have grown up and started out for themselves they
can go as far away as they want for food. There is no
longer any need for their parents to protect the supply
close to home. So the fathers sing less and less. By the
end of July, you hardly ever hear them except now and
then in the early morning or toward evening.

There are other reasons, too, for this gradual end to
bird singing. One is that the high spirits of spring and
the excitement of having a family have worn themselves
out. By this time the old birds begin to relax. Also, summer is the time when they shed their worn-out feathers
and grow new ones to replace them. This seems to leave
them feeling grumpy. When it's over, and they are all
fitted out in new feathers, they seem to feel better. So,
in late August and even September, you sometimes hear

snatches of the old spring songs. But these are always shorter and quieter—hardly more than echoes of the cheery music that filled the air only a few months earlier.

Perhaps you have seen several pairs of *different species* of birds nesting quite near each other. A year or two ago, on my own place, a chipping sparrow had a nest in a low bush only fifteen feet from a house wren's. A family of towhees lived about forty feet in the opposite direction. A pair of robins nested in an apple tree on one side of the lawn. And two red-eyed vireos had their nest in a small maple on the other side. All five pairs raised strong, healthy families. None of them had any trouble finding plenty of food.

Eastern
meadowlark

The song of the meadowlark is one of the loveliest.

All About Birds

Yet we know that each pair of birds needs to protect a certain amount of space against others of its own kind. Then how can so many different kinds of birds live peacefully in such a limited area?

The answer is simple. Each bird species has certain favorite foods which it likes better than others. Robins devour earthworms from the lawn. Also they are crazy about small fruits, rather large smooth grubs and many insects big enough to be worth grabbing. Towhees like some of these things, too. But usually they look for them among and under bushes instead of in open places as the robins do.

Chipping sparrows are also ground feeders. They poke and scratch around in the grass where they can catch little bugs, grubs and seeds that neither towhees nor robins bother with to any extent. As for the wrens, they specialize in many kinds of little caterpillars and other small insects. They find these by skipping in and out of odd corners which most other birds pass by. And the vireos catch their small insects among the upper branches of the trees.

Do you see how it works? Each type of bird chooses its special kinds of foods, or it goes hunting in particular places that other types don't use. That is why all five

A robin will tug and pull to get an earthworm out of the ground.

of these neighboring pairs found as much as they and their young could eat. But you can be very sure that if a second pair of any of these species had tried to move into that little piece of ground there would have been a battle.

One of the best things about this whole matter of birds singing in the spring, and the reasons for it, is that you can actually hear and see it going on all around you. Many of the songs are really musical and well worth listening to. And it's always fun to hear a strange one and learn what kind of bird sings it. Very often, too, a song is a tip-off that there's a nest not far away, and you may be able to find it.

Nests for Everybody

Many, many kinds of wild creatures, from birds to wasps, ants, fish and squirrels, make nests in which to raise their young families. Some of these homes are so cozy that you wouldn't mind living there yourself if you were small enough. The trouble with many of them is that they are so few and far between, or so perfectly hidden, that they are hard to locate except by accident.

Those which the birds build, though, are fairly easy to find. There are dozens and dozens of different sizes, shapes and styles of nests. Often you will wonder how their builders ever managed to put them together so neatly.

Birds have only three nest-building tools: their own bills, feet and bodies. With the first two they gather the materials and put them together. The last often serves as a mold for shaping the inside of the nest. This is the way a bird makes sure that the nest will fit perfectly when the old bird settles down in it to brood the eggs.

This is surprisingly simple equipment, yet birds are able to weave baskets, dig holes, chop wood, plaster on mud, construct platforms and caves, build roofs, make soft mattresses, and fetch all the stuff they need for such jobs. But birds know exactly how to use the tools they have, and their finished work is much better than ours would be if we tried to imitate them. They never need to be taught what to do, either. Their ancestors have been building nests in the same way for so many generations that today every bird knows the methods without studying them.

All the birds of any one species build the same kind of nest in the same general way. When an expert naturalist finds a nest, he can be almost sure what kind of bird made it. Every Baltimore oriole weaves a strong hanging pouch for a nest. It is made of plant fibers, soft inner tree bark and often bits of string. This pear-shaped nest hangs from the slender end of a tree branch.

Several kinds of vireos use the same sorts of material that the orioles like. However, their nests are cuplike. They generally hang where a small branch forks into two arms.

Sparrows, on the other hand, use stiffer, grassy stuff and tiny rootlets. They carry these building materials to a hidden, twiggy spot in a low bush or vine, or right on the ground. There they cleverly shape them into

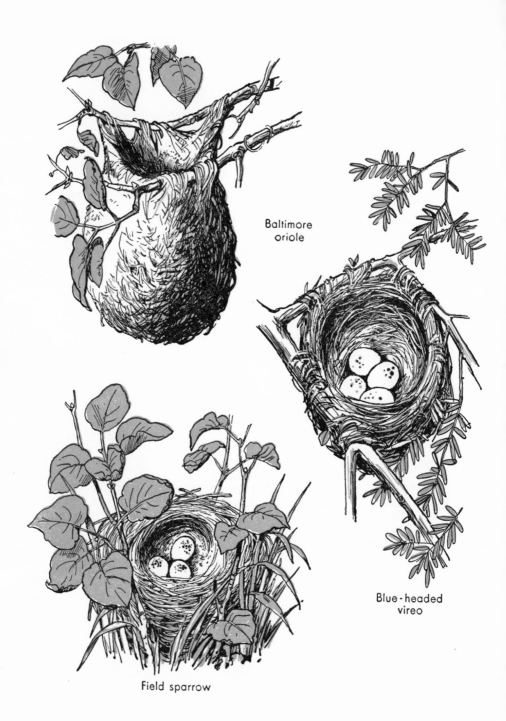

Baltimore
oriole

Blue-headed
vireo

Field sparrow

Birds have three nest-building tools: their bills, feet and bodies.

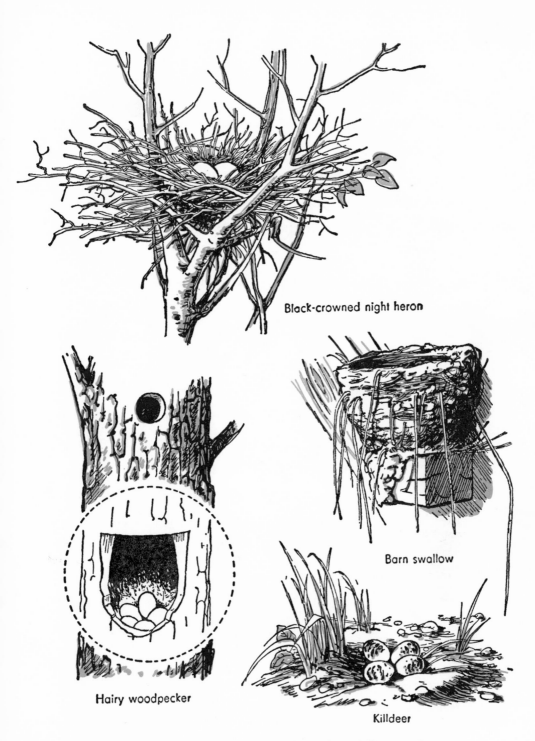

Black-crowned night heron

Barn swallow

Hairy woodpecker

Killdeer

They build nests of many materials and in different shapes.

thick bowls which are supported from below instead of being hung by their rims.

Robins and wood thrushes choose more or less the same sort of material that the sparrows do. First they pick out a good location, usually in the crotch of a tree. Sometimes robins will choose a flat ledge around a porch or some building. Then they gather bits of twigs and dry grass and plaster them together with mud which they bring in their bills.

Phoebes and barn swallows are good mud masons, too. But wrens, bluejays, doves and herons generally use twigs with maybe a few softer things here and there.

Bank swallows and kingfishers have a different method. They build at the end of long tunnels which they peck and scrape into steep banks. And woodpeckers chop out their homes in tree trunks or limbs. Often they hollow out holes big enough to accommodate a family of at least five or six. Nuthatches and chickadees often do the same thing when they find a dead stub that is old enough and soft enough for them to work on successfully. Some of the sea and shore birds surprise you by scratching little hollows in the sand or even laying their eggs on bare, hard ground. The same thing is done by the long-winged nighthawk you sometimes see chasing insects high up in the summer evening sky.

Most birds that build regular nests give them very soft linings. This is to help keep the eggs warm and protect them from breakage. Sometimes it's hard to find enough of the right material for this. Wild geese and ducks pluck off the very soft feathers from their own breasts and stomachs and use them to give their eggs wonderfully comfortable down "mattresses." This curious habit has another important advantage. It thins out the dense plumage of the mother bird. Then the eggs can come into direct contact with her skin as she sits on them. This is a great help in successful incubation.

Very few of the birds that are likely to be around your yard, or in the neighborhood, start nesting until the first daffodils are in bloom. Their busiest season begins when the tree leaves start coming out, and it continues for six weeks or more.

During this time, if you watch closely, you may see a half-dozen different kinds of birds gathering nesting materials. They pick them up in their beaks and fly off with them to the hidden spots they have already chosen for their new homes. If you can follow very slowly and quietly, you may catch a glimpse of them actually building the nest. But it is better not to go near, for the birds will almost certainly be frightened and move somewhere else. You see, they want safety for the new families more than anything else. And so they do their best to keep the locations of their nests a deep secret.

You can have a lot of fun, during this nesting season, by putting handfuls of their favorite building supplies in the branches of shrubs or on the ground at the edge of the lawn. Or try placing them in an open wire basket nailed on top of a short post. Sooner or later, some bird will find the treasure. Then others will discover it and show you more fluttering antics than you have ever dreamed of.

Excellent materials for such a project are wads of thistledown or cotton; bits of dried moss; soft shreds from the outside of big weed stalks, or strips of the inner bark of a dead cedar tree; six-inch pieces of soft string or knitting yarn; dead grass leaves; small twigs; hair groomed from the manes or tails of horses (cut these into four-inch pieces so the birds won't get tangled in them and perhaps be injured); and clippings from long-haired dogs such as poodles and collies. And of course, you should have plenty of fluffy feathers, particularly white ones from the breasts and sides of chickens or ducks. Several kinds of birds like to add a few such feathers to their nests. When one blows away from them on a windy day, they go almost crazy chasing it.

It is hard to get together a supply of such things in a hurry. For that reason, it's a good idea to collect them whenever you have a chance and store them in a tight box until nesting time. Almost anything that is in small, soft pieces will be good. You will find many kinds once you start looking for them.

For another interesting project, you may want to collect different kinds of used nests so that you can study them. Of course no one should approach a nest while it is being built. Even after the eggs have been laid, anything more than a quick look inside once in a while is likely to scare away the parent birds. But there is very little chance that a nest will be used again after the young ones have left. So there is no reason why you should not collect it then. The best time is after the leaves have fallen in autumn. Then you will be able to find many more nests than during the summer.

The Story of Eggs

Of all the wonders of the bird world, the eggs are probably the most interesting. A few of them are only half an inch long while others are four or five times that size. But inside these smooth, rounded little packages there is everything needed to make brand-new birds exactly like their parents. Even a food supply for the youngsters is there too—enough to last until they are big enough to hatch out into the open air.

A great many kinds of eggs are as pretty as jewels, too, with shells that show just about every color you can think of. Some are spotted at one end or all over, and some are covered with scrawly markings that run this way and that. Others are solid blue, greenish, yellowish, white, brown and even pink. And a few kinds have four or five different colors all in the same shell.

But these are not the only surprises. All the eggs laid by any one species of bird look practically the same. But in many cases a careful examination will show that no two of the four or five in some particular nest are exactly like each other. One might have more dots than its neighbor, or its color might be a shade darker, or something like that.

Most of these colors and markings come from many little glands or "paint cans" inside the mother bird. Some of them, particularly the plain solid colors like robin's-egg blue, are built into the shell while it is being formed. However, scratchy markings of different colors, such as you see on the eggs of an oriole or a red-winged blackbird, are only on the outside of the shell. They make uneven lines or blobs because the egg itself moved a little while the "paint" was being put on.

And here is something else.

Birds' eggs, even the hens' eggs that you buy at the grocery store, are more pointed at one end than the other. Sometimes this difference is really noticeable. Again it may be so slight that you can hardly see it. But it is almost always there.

The pointed end is the one that comes out of the

mother bird first. There are several reasons for its shape. One is that it makes the egg easier to lay. Another is that such a pointed end is stronger than a more rounded one. So there is less chance that the shell will break if the egg happens to land on a hard surface when it is laid.

And for a third reason, pointed eggs are less likely to roll out of a shallow nest or off a rock ledge which some sea birds choose for their nests. If you want to see what happens to an egg on a flat surface, try this experiment. Roll a hen's egg and a small round ball gently along a bare floor or the level top of a table, and note the different courses they take. The ball will roll away in a straight line, but the pointed egg will either wobble or circle back toward its starting place.

Most of the land birds that you see from day to day lay from four to six eggs in a "clutch," or nestful. Quite a number do this twice or occasionally three times every season. Bobwhites have the unusual habit of laying a single clutch of fifteen or so. Duck families are often as big as the bobwhite's. But a hummingbird lays only two eggs, and gannets are perfectly satisfied with a single egg each year. And an albatross usually lays exactly one egg every two years!

Generally the different eggs in a clutch are laid two

or more days apart. The mother bird does not start incubating, or sitting on them, until the last one is in the nest. She has a good reason for this, of course. It is the warmth of her body that makes the little birds start growing inside their shells. If she began sitting on the first egg as soon as she laid it, her body heat would give that particular one a head start. None of the later eggs would ever catch up. This would mean that each young bird would be a different age and size. The oldest and biggest would take so much of the food that the smaller ones wouldn't get enough to keep them growing properly. To keep this from happening no bird is given a head start in the beginning.

The barn owl is the one strange exception to this rule about waiting for a full clutch. It nests in old abandoned buildings, tree hollows, church steeples and many other peculiar hide-outs. This big night bird sometimes has a clutch of as many as eight eggs, and it starts sitting on the first one as soon as it's laid. When the last one hatches, all the youngsters are of different ages and sizes, as is usually the case in human families. Don't ask me why a mother barn owl does this, for I couldn't tell you! Nor could anybody else, as far as I know.

In the nest of a barn owl there will be babies of all sizes.

Nearly all these matters we've been talking about take place in every occupied bird nest that you find. For the sake of the owners' family, it's best to keep away from the nest until all the eggs have been laid and the old bird is incubating them. If you looked at them before then, or should touch them at *any* time, the parents might desert the nest and start one somewhere else. The best plan is to take no more than an occasional short peek while the old bird is away from the nest getting a few minutes' vacation from her sitting job.

As soon as the eggs hatch, the old birds carry the empty shells away and drop them far from the nest.

This is done so that no hungry fox or other creature that happened to see them would get the idea that there must be some tasty young birds near by. You will often find these empty shells lying on the ground, and it's fun to figure out what kind of bird they belonged to. Many of the books about identifying birds describe the eggs of each species, and you will find these a real help in learning to recognize them yourself. Probably the best way is to start a collection of your own.

This, then, is the story of eggs, cut down to its most important facts. There will be a great deal more to learn about it later on, of course, for eggs are really amazing things. And so are the baby birds that begin life inside them.

When Birds Are Very Young

In the case of most small land birds, the incubation period lasts for twelve to eighteen days. The time depends on the species. The general rule is that the larger the species the longer its eggs take to hatch. In fact, really big ones like eagles have to keep their eggs warm for many weeks before the infants inside them grow large and strong enough to break out of their shells.

All About Birds

How do young birds escape from their eggshell prisons when the right time comes? Why, each one just keeps pushing and pecking away at the inside of its shell until it finally cracks open. This is hard work for a wobbly baby chick that has never seen daylight, but in the case of a great many species the small struggler has a special tool to work with. It is called an egg tooth, and it looks like a hard, sharp little point on the tip of the upper mandible. This is a real help in cutting through the shell. But after the egg tooth has done its work and the little fellow is out in the air, it soon disappears.

It is very important for a young bird to grow up fast and become able to take care of itself. For this reason the parents start feeding it as soon as it dries off after breaking out of the shell. In most cases its food is the same as the old birds eat, but they prepare it for infant mouths by pulling or crushing it into pieces small enough for the youngsters to swallow. Various insects and soft caterpillars are especially popular among the birds you are likely to see around home, and so are scraps of ripe berries.

The babies digest their food so rapidly that they always seem to be hungry for more. This keeps their

The nest of the barn swallow may be high in the rafters.

parents steadily at work finding enough to keep the small stomachs filled. It's not at all unusual for a family of young wrens to be fed four or five hundred times between dawn and dusk. No wonder they are strong enough to fly when they are only a couple of weeks old!

This plan of fast eating and growing doesn't always work, unfortunately, and for a reason you'd never expect. It has to do with a certain kind of small blackbird, known as a cowbird, which never builds a nest of its own. Instead, when laying time comes, the female cowbird looks for other small birds' nests. Here she will drop her eggs when the real owners aren't looking. Then she sneaks away and lets the foster parents incubate her eggs along with their own.

Now, this mean trick might not be so bad except for certain curious facts. First, the rightful owners usually do not notice that the cowbird egg is different from theirs. They go right ahead and give it the best of care. Secondly, the young cowbird hatches in ten days—more quickly than other birds. Because it hatches first, it is stronger and hungrier than the birds that belong in the nest. It soon grabs most of the food that is brought. Often this means that most or all of the rightful occupants of the nest are either starved or pushed over the edge by the greedy stranger long before they can take care of themselves.

Generally a cowbird lays only one egg in any particular nest, for she seems to like spreading them around. In a single season she may produce ten or a dozen of them, so she really stirs up a lot of trouble.

While young birds are still in the nest, they are unable to fly to a safer place in case of danger, of course. Only their parents can protect them. And the ways they do it are really something to watch! When some enemy threatens, the mother will try to attract his attention from the nest of baby birds. Some kinds of birds, especially those that build on or near the ground, will flop around close to the nest. In order to coax the enemy away from their helpless offspring, they pretend to be badly wounded and easy to catch. Often the mother gives such a good imitation of being crippled that the prowling dog, fox or cat can't help making a dive for her. But somehow she always manages to keep just out of reach. Gradually she leads her pursuer on and on to a safe distance from the nest. Then, suddenly recovering from her imitation injury, she flies away as strong as ever. Finally she circles back to her waiting family.

You are likely to see this trick played almost anywhere during the early summer while young birds are still in their nests or have just left them. Someday a mother bird will try it on you, too, and you'll marvel at what a perfect actress she is.

Another good lifesaver for infant birds, or even eggs, is for the parents to make a noisy fuss when a possible enemy comes anywhere near the nest. Most of the other birds in the neighborhood quickly join in such a row. Their combined chirps, squawks and even dive-bombings are enough to confuse and even drive the prowler away. Perhaps you will hear such a roughhouse going on in the garden or among the shrubs at the end of the yard. If so, be sure to creep up quietly and watch it. I don't know of any more interesting proof of how much

These young kingbirds are almost big enough to leave the nest.

the safety of their families means to parent birds.

Finally the time comes when the youngsters' wing feathers are pretty well grown. Soon you will notice them scrambling around restlessly in the nest. Sometimes they will stretch their wings as if to see how they work. Usually the parents flutter about near by as though to encourage them. Pretty soon the little fellows take off and do surprisingly well for a first attempt. Sometimes they all jump into the air at once. Or they may leave singly a few minutes apart. If one timid little fellow hesitates too long, his parents will jabber encouragement to him. Sometimes they almost push him over the edge of the nest.

A few days later the new family will be flying strongly and catching most of its own food. Young birds learn their important lessons fast. But almost never do they return to the abandoned nest, even at night or during a storm.

A great many kinds of birds have special alarm calls which they use at all times of the year and long after the youngsters are on their own. The purpose seems to be to warn everybody that there's something dangerous around. And here is a queer thing about it: although each species has its own particular warning cry, all the other kinds seem to understand it. The best alarm-sounders of all are generally the bluejays, robins, catbirds, wood thrushes and crows.

These are some of the important ways in which birds protect their families, themselves and often their neighbors. There are many more that you will come across from time to time, as you learn more about birds. It's a good idea to keep a notebook in which to write down some of these bird habits. Under such headings as "Defense," "Attack," "Hide," "Dodge," "Sit Tight," and

All About Birds

"Make a Break for It," list just what you have seen and *what kind of bird was doing it*. After a while you will have a very unusual sort of record. It will be a great help in really understanding the lives of the birds around you.

There's No Place Like Home

Several years ago I knew a Baltimore oriole that never could sing the way he was supposed to do. Usually these handsome birds will sing three or four notes as they fly around among the trees. This fellow said nothing but *whee-ee*, with a sort of gulp in the middle as though he had something stuck in his throat. Whatever his trouble may have been, it didn't keep him from finding a mate. The pair of them raised a fine, healthy family in a bag-like nest hung at the tip of a long elm branch over our driveway.

I had never known an oriole with a voice like that. So when we heard the same queer song the next spring, we felt sure that our old friend had flown back to Connecticut from his winter vacation in Central America. Maybe he had the same mate, or maybe she was a new one. We never did find out about that. But soon there

The male Baltimore oriole is a brilliant orange and black.

was another nest in the big elm, and another brood of little Baltimore orioles. He returned the following year, too, and helped bring up another family. Then something serious must have happened to him, for we never heard his unusual song again.

Here was one particular oriole, you see, that spent at least three seasons in the same section and among the same trees. He flew two thousand miles or more each spring to get back to them. Why he chose this one spot, I have no idea, for there were dozens of others just as good within a mile or so. Maybe those trees really meant home to him, in some mysterious way that nobody understands.

All About Birds

A great many migratory birds return in this way to the neighborhoods where they had grown up as youngsters or perhaps had nested the year before. Sometimes you can recognize one of them by its peculiar song, like our oriole. Or maybe your bird has some white feathers where there ought to be dark ones—a kind of unnatural coloring, called *mutation*, that happens now and then. A friend of mine was able to identify a certain catbird for several seasons because it had a badly crooked left leg, probably the result of some accident.

The other day I was reading a lot of records published by the Bird Banding Association. This is a group of people who put little numbered aluminum rings on the legs of wild birds. This is done as a way of finding out where birds go in their travels, how long they live, and things like that. Some of these bands are attached to young birds before they leave the nest. Others are fastened to old ones which have been caught alive in special traps which cannot hurt them. When a band is put on, a record is made of when and where it was put on, and on what kind of bird. So, when a banded bird is found or trapped at some later time, the banders can check back and learn a lot about its history.

This banding work has been going on for years. It

doesn't bother the birds in the least, but it has taught us a great deal about where they go. Here are some of the facts I found while I was reading about it. All of them are about species that migrate regularly to the south in autumn and north again in spring. The bands were put on them near where they nested, and each year they were trapped at the same places so that their numbers could be checked.

One pair of crested flycatchers returned for three years in a row. Five young catbirds came back regularly for the next four years. Two wood thrushes flew back home every spring for five years. Six house wrens returned for three seasons, and a purple grackle for four. A partly albino robin set a record by showing up at the same place every spring for nine years! You can be very sure that these proved cases are only a small fraction of all the birds of many kinds that come back after the winter to the places where they were hatched or in which they had raised families of their own.

Yes, this sort of coming home is a pretty wonderful thing to be able to do. It seems still more remarkable when you remember that migration trips are often made at night when the birds can't see clearly where they are going. Nobody knows for sure how they find their way, and perhaps we will never learn that particular secret. But ornithologists are not going to stop searching for the answer.

One suggestion has been made that birds may have a "sense of direction" which guides them. Perhaps it is like that of a dog that finds its way home after being lost a long distance away. Another theory is that birds follow the courses of big north-and-south rivers like the Mississippi and the Ohio. Large numbers of them certainly do this. But what about all those others that fly back to regions where there are no such streams? And

Crested flycatchers will often come back year after year.

a third idea is that there may be some gadget in a bird's brain, or some other part of it, that is affected by magnetic or other waves from the earth or in the atmosphere. This makes it possible to steer a course by them. For all we know, birds may be able to "come in on a beam" like the pilot of a plane when he flies by instrument.

Whatever the real explanation may be, you can be sure that many birds *do* return as though they believed that there's no place like home.

Very likely this will happen in your neighborhood, too, so be on the watch for the home-comers. You can recognize them by their unnatural voices, off-color feathers, crooked legs, little metal bands on their ankles, or anything else that marks them as being different from their fellows.

More Birds Around Home

While you're watching for birds that return year after year, you may want to make your neighborhood a still more pleasant place for birds to come to at *all* times of the year.

Does your home have a little ground around it—

maybe some lawn, a few shrubs and trees, perhaps a garden? You can easily make it an even better place for wild birds, and so have many more chances to watch them close-up.

The things that attract birds most quickly are food, drinking and bathing water, and thick bushes, vines and trees which will provide shelter for them and plenty of good nesting places. You can help supply each of these needs.

As you already know, birds eat a tremendous number of different foods. Some of these, particularly small insects, they find among the leaves and branches of big and little plants. Thus, the more of these you have the better the birds will like it. Usually insects are plentiful for bird food in warm weather. But they are likely to be scarce in fall and winter. In those seasons you can attract hungry birds from quite a distance simply by putting out ready-made meals for them in convenient places.

Favorite foods are stale bread crumbs, seeds of sunflower, millet and hemp, very finely cracked corn, peanut butter and pieces of beef suet from the butcher's. Birds enjoy these foods right through the year, but especially in winter. All of them can be bought at bird and poultry feed stores except for the crumbs, suet and peanut butter. It is a good idea to get a small box of cage-bird gravel, too, which will help your visitors digest their meals.

You can scatter some of the food right on the ground as long as there is no snow to cover it up. However, you usually get a better view of the birds if you put the food in special feeders placed where you can see them easily from your windows. Many kinds of these feeders are sold in stores that have garden seeds and supplies. But you may want to have the fun of building your own according to the plans and directions given on page 126.

All wild birds must have fresh, clean water to drink and bathe in. In fact, there is no better way to attract birds in warm weather than by keeping a supply of water ready for them. It is well to keep a good-sized shallow basin of water in an open spot. The birds will be particularly pleased if it is near some bushes in which they can perch while drying their feathers or hide quickly from a cat or some other sudden danger. It is rather hard to make a really fine bird bath that will last a long time. Eventually you may decide to get one at a store. But for a while the birds will get great pleasure from water in an ordinary metal wash basin or shallow

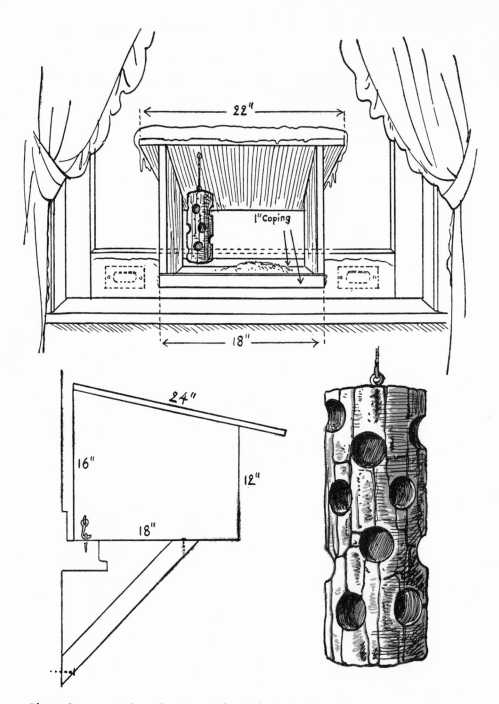

Plans for a window feeder with stick to hold suet or peanut butter.

dishpan. If it is set in a hollow of the ground there is less danger of tipping over. You will find that you need to change the water at least once a day to be sure it is fresh.

When it comes to plants for safe shelter and nesting places, most of the shrubs that people plant to make their home grounds attractive will please the birds, too. Some of the best fairly small ones are lilac, barberry, mock orange, forsythia, climbing and "bush" honeysuckles, ramblers and other kinds of climbing roses, privet, yew, arborvitae and spirea.

Hawthorn, dogwood, flowering crabapple, red cedar and holly are favorite medium-size trees. Many birds like to eat their berries as well as nest and roost among their branches. As for larger trees, maples, elms, oaks, pines, spruces and hemlocks are some of the best.

Another great attraction for birds is a good, thick pile of brush in some out-of-the-way corner. It will be a favorite spot for small winter birds such as juncos and sparrows. These hardy little fellows will climb up and down among the dry twigs until they find the ones that suit them best. They will even sleep in your brush pile night after night. By piling on a few more branches every fall, to make up for those older ones which have rotted away at the bottom, you can keep one of these piles going for years.

As I said, all of the living plants we've been talking about provide good nesting spots for many kinds of birds, including robins, thrushes, catbirds, thrashers, warblers, several sparrows, orioles, tanagers, grosbeaks, mockingbirds, cardinals and even hummingbirds. But when it comes to raising a family they mean little or nothing to bluebirds, house wrens, chickadees, flickers, crested flycatchers, tree swallows, purple martins, nuthatches and screech owls. These birds prefer to build their nests in holes. You can attract them as neighbors by making and putting up special nest boxes.

Cypress, white pine or redwood boards 7/8″ thick are the best material from which to build nest boxes, but almost any kind of wood will do if it is between 3/4″ and 1″ thick and has no cracks. Screws are better than nails for fastening the pieces together, because they will stay tight for years. In any case they ought to be 1½″ long and of medium thickness.

On page 129 you will see plans for a bluebird nest box. If you are going to build a box, be sure to follow the measurements exactly. And before you put it together, cover the edges and both sides of every piece

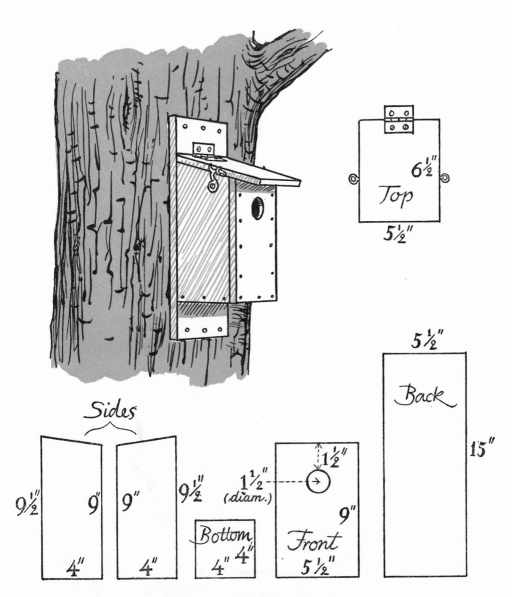

Top

6½″

5½″

Back

5½″

15″

Sides

9½″ 9″ 9″ 9½″

4″ 4″

Bottom

4″ 4″

Front

1½″

1½″ (diam.)

9″

5½″

Plans for a bluebird nest box

with brown or gray wood stain or paint and let it dry thoroughly. This will make the box last longer when it's outside in all sorts of weather.

There are special reasons for that hinged top and the hook on each side to hold it shut. Birds never throw out their old nests when they have finished using them; they just fly off and leave everything behind. However, they like to have a clean place to start a new one, so it's a good idea for you to do the cleaning up yourself as soon as the young birds have flown. This is easy to do when you can raise the hinged top and pull out all the twigs, grass and other material. Another reason for the movable roof is that it gives you a chance to peek in once in a while after the eggs hatch and see how the young family is getting along.

Nest boxes are generally nailed to tree trunks, large

Wild birds like to have fresh water to drink and bathe in.

branches or the tops of posts six to ten feet from the ground. Those intended for chickadees and nuthatches should be in heavily shaded places, since these birds naturally nest in woods and like dark homes. But if you want bluebirds, wrens, crested flycatchers, flickers or screech owls, choose spots that face open spaces such as a lawn or garden and are shaded during the hot hours of the day. As you might expect of birds that practically live on the wing, tree swallows and purple martins like houses right out in the wide open spaces.

Accidents Will Happen

When you remember how frail birds are, it's a wonder that they are so successful in keeping out of serious trouble. I suppose that practically every one of them, at least once and probably many times in its life, escapes death only by inches or seconds. Generally the danger is not one that we could have prevented even if we had seen it coming. On the other hand, there are times when you *can* help a wild bird that's out of luck, and maybe save its life.

The young bird that has tumbled out of its nest before it can fly is one that you can help. If most of its feathers are quite well grown and if it is able to stand up, the best plan is to put it back in the nest. If this is impossible, lift it carefully into a bush or low tree where it can sit on a branch and be out of reach of dogs and cats. Its parents are almost certain to be near by. They will quickly find and feed it, so its worst troubles will be over.

Several times, when there were no bushes around, I have built a 5-foot pen of poultry wire around such a youngster. Then I have stuck some leafy branches into the ground to give shade from the hot sun. The old birds will take care of their babe until it can fly, perhaps in a day or two.

Once in a while a heavy storm blows down a nest full of young birds—a much more serious accident. If you find such a nest, put it back in place, family and all. Maybe you will have to tie it together so it will last until the little fellows are old enough to leave. If the nest is too badly broken for this, you might try making an imitation nest out of dead grass and other soft stuff. Put it where the real one had been, and place the young birds in it. In such cases the parents will probably continue taking care of their family as though nothing had happened.

Helpless young birds that have lost their parents for some reason need your help badly. Certainly, their feathered neighbors will pay no attention to them. You will find that the job of raising them yourself won't be easy, but it's worth trying.

First, get a good-sized cardboard box, maybe a shoe box, and put a few handfuls of dead grass or scraps of torn paper in one corner for a nest. You will also need a piece of cloth to cover the box at night and keep out drafts and cold air. This can be the orphans' home until they are old enough to fly.

An excellent food for most of these baby birds is a

A baby bird should be fed every half-hour from dawn to dark.

mixture of hard-boiled egg yolks and fine bread crumbs mashed together and dampened with a little milk. Canned dog food and small scraps of chopped raw beef are good, too. So are very small pieces of fresh fruit. Drinking water will not be needed; indeed, it is dangerous for young birds until they are old enough to drink by themselves.

A young bird should be fed at least once every half-hour from early morning until dark. If it is less than a week old, it will probably open its mouth when it hears you coming. All you need do is to pick up a scrap of food on the tip of a very small wooden spoon, a soft little paintbrush, or the flat end of a wooden toothpick, and carefully place it well down in that waiting throat. When your patient stops opening its mouth, you'll know that it has had enough for a while.

Older youngsters are often so frightened by their new home that at first they will not open their mouths to be fed. In this case pick up each one gently in your left hand with its back against your palm and your fingers curved loosely around its breast. In this way you can hold its wings against its sides. In this position the neck and head will be in the crotch between your thumb and first finger. Generally the bird will clutch one of your

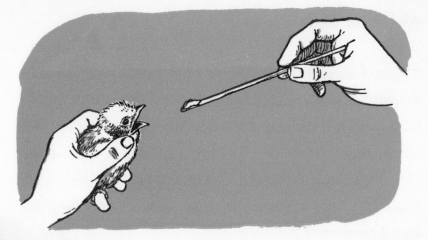

Hold the bird gently with its back against your palm.

other fingers and crouch there quietly. With the tips of your left thumb and forefinger, press lightly against the sides of its bill, away back at the base. The mouth will open enough for your right hand to place the food down in the throat.

Sometimes this force-feeding, as it is called, will work even on grown-up birds which, for one reason or another, are half starved and in need of emergency treatment. Generally, however, it is better to put the patient in a good-sized, wire-covered box and scatter the food on the bottom where he can pick it up himself. Such a bird is likely to be cold when you find him, so be sure that the box is kept in a warm, quiet place until he regains his strength.

A box like this is a fine place for the bird that has knocked itself out by flying against a glass window or the wire screening of a porch. If its skull is crushed, or any blood shows around the bill or eyes, the injury is probably too serious to be helped by any treatment. But many times a few hours' rest in a dark box with plenty of air holes will make the victim as well as ever.

What about the bird with a broken wing or leg? I'm afraid that such cases are almost hopeless, for there is no sure way of keeping the injured part motionless long enough for the broken bone to grow together. Even if the bone should finally knit, the bird is likely to be so crippled that it cannot get around safely outdoors. Of course, you might be able to take care of it for a time in a cage. But wild birds love to be free, and it's really not fair to keep them in captivity unless that is the only possible way of saving their lives.

Index

Index

Index